FRENCH KITCHEN LESSONS

CAT BUDE

FRENCH KITCHEN LESSONS

Recipes & Stories *from*
Normandy's Rabbit Hill Farm

Hardie Grant

NORTH AMERICA

CONTENTS

RECIPES

HOW IS IT THAT SUCH A HUMBLE ROOM as a kitchen can bring so much comfort, steadfast security, and necessary consistency? A haven. A place where some of life's most important decisions are explored and made or sometimes questioned. A room of function and almost constant activity and yet a place of rest.

Somewhere, there is a photo of me sitting on the floor of our kitchen when our home in Normandy was new to us, surveying the removal of baseboards in the empty box of a room that would someday be filled with shelves of porcelain and racks of copper pots. The walls would soon hear whispers and laughter, just as they had for over three hundred years. Broken tiles would continue to hold weight. The light would shine through the tall windowpanes in a magical way, healing us even on the hardest days or adding brightness to every celebration.

At the time, I really had no idea what this kitchen would become. White walls, high ceilings with robust ancient beams holding them up, and colorful tiles smoothed by countless transits across them. I fell instantly in love with this kitchen, this space that would hold our family and dearest friends. I fell in love with her even before I had cooked a single dish of food.

We found an ancient hardwood butcher's counter that we outfitted with an inexpensive prep sink. We repaired the old white walls and refreshed them with glossy white paint. We scrubbed, and we fixed, and we picnicked sitting on the floor, surrounded by boxes.

We opened our hearts and allowed ourselves to dream about the possibilities of this maybe crazy decision to uproot ourselves from a life we knew and loved, to start all over again in the safety of this kitchen. There was not just one time but many in the months after we found our new French country life, that we eagerly moved forward toward a future we had only dreamed about—one that at times still defies definition.

Today, I stand in this room, still amazed that after choosing this home so many years ago, that the kitchen would become my place in such a significant way. When I travel, it's the first room I return to. Not the bedroom to unpack my bags, or the living room to crash down on the sofa and begin to battle the jet lag, but the kitchen. Most likely, I will reach for the closest tea towel to wipe down something that got overlooked during my absence—that's just the way I am. But I will also stand quietly, absorbing the room's spirits, its calming energy, and, of course, the light.

A kitchen is more than a room. It's a sacred space that holds you and the hearts and souls of every person who steps in and gathers there to be nurtured and nourished.

To this day, this kitchen allows me to be pushed and to grow, to accept and to carry on, to heal and to believe. Food is prepared there with intention and love . . . to feed, to teach, to share, and also for celebration. Daily life and the stunning seasonal light are captured in photographs and shared for inspiration and even encouragement. What I give to this kitchen and this home and what I create within its walls give back to me beyond measure. So perhaps this book, in a way, is a love letter to a kitchen. It is, undeniably, a love letter to a life.

INTRODUCTION

HAVE YOU ALWAYS DREAMED OF LIVING in France? That is the question that comes up most frequently when I meet someone new. If it's not that question, then it's a funnier one: Did you always dream of marrying a Frenchman? My answers? Not really and no. That's especially true, since first meeting my now-husband at a dog park in Brentwood, California, I was convinced that the man I had met—with his very timid yet sweet, rescued Australian shepherd—was German. Apparently, I am less than astute about identifying accents; in fact, we spoke for several hours before I realized he was French. Although we barely spent a day apart after that first meeting, we didn't discuss living in France until long after we were married and many years into our American West Coast life.

It's not that we had never contemplated living in my husband's mother country, it's just that during that phase of our lives, we felt quite firmly planted on Bainbridge Island, near Seattle, Washington, with our family of four, and a fifth on the way. We both felt that our wandering and adventurous souls seemed finally to be at rest. As a couple, we had moved more than a dozen times, relishing new beginnings. We became weekend warriors, with home and garden projects always lined up, dinner parties scheduled, and school events to attend. A business. A home. Settled in. Despite all this, in June 2010, we made the decision to move to France, where a new adventure lay ahead.

We arrived at my husband's parents' home with our two children, three cats, three dogs, and lots of luggage. We lived there for three months in their tall five-bedroom house in Deauville, a coastal town in lower Normandy. Those months passed in a blur. I felt as if my jet lag never went away, and I began to realize I was feeling more hesitant than hopeful. A culture feels entirely different when you switch from being a tourist to a transplant. So, I decided to give the entire plan just two years, and then I would pack up our little family and head back to the safety of a country and culture that I was intimately familiar with.

During those first few months, there were few places where I felt at home. My mind and heart still lingered on that little creaky-floored farmhouse we had left behind in the Pacific Northwest, with its tiny kitchen decked with worn copper countertops and the sound of the screen door banging shut when our boys rushed through.

In this new setting and unfamiliar country, I tried to get my bearings. I sought out the rare places where I felt welcomed and normal. As it turned out, the open market—a requisite part of daily life in France—soon became one of those places. The vendors were friendly, tolerating my fumbling attempts to speak French and greeting me each time with welcoming gestures. It was a place where I could benefit from my extensive French food vocabulary, even if I couldn't conjugate a verb correctly.

Routines and rituals are an important part of French culture: the daily trips to the markets, the long five-course lunches, and the common practice of taking a break in the middle of the day. During that first summer at my in-laws' home, I would come downstairs in the morning on any given day to find my father-in-law in the kitchen preparing lunch at just after ten o'clock, having already gone to the market and making his rounds to the butcher and boulangerie. His trip included not only getting the essential ingredients for that day's lunch but also catching up on the news and events of the day with his lifelong friends.

My father-in-law, referred to in French as *beau-père* and called Papi by family members, had been a professional chef and had maintained longtime relationships with every vendor and producer that he had ever met. So, needless to say, his daily rounds were thorough and very social.

Even before I descended the last level of stairs, I would be hit with the aroma of stocks boiling, meats roasting, and vegetables steaming. On the table would be a carefully curated mise en place; my father-in-law's organization made use of every surface in that very small kitchen. The TV would be on, with no one watching it, and he would most likely be humming as he cut baguettes into thick slices and sipped his first whiskey of the day.

One of the main reasons we had moved to France was to be near my in-laws—to be able to have the time with my husband's parents and to be there to support them in their retirement. Keep in mind, too, that we arrived in France without jobs or a place to live, with a new baby on the way, and with very little money. And despite or because of those circumstances, we needed to find a HOME. Looking back, I realize how precious, albeit difficult, it was to be able to live with my in-laws for those months.

Toward the end of that first summer in France, after a brief yet discouraging search for a rental, we found a small 1940s brick house near a beach in a tiny town ten minutes from my in-laws. The house was bland, with terrible rhubarb-colored wallpaper, a closet-sized

kitchen, and no garden. But it was a quick five-minute walk to a steep staircase that brought you to a dramatic rocky beach that, on most days between September and July, was completely deserted. After moving in, my morning routine very quickly included long walks or slow jogs down the beach. We made the most of our time in that house, despite being closely governed by our ninety-year-old landlady, who would often peek in the windows and leave scolding notes on our door. All of that changed, however, after the birth of our daughter, when she presented us with a carefully knitted, fuzzy cardigan, and all was forgiven.

I made the best of living in that house, trading a driveway for a potager garden and, thanks to inspirational trips to local markets and farms, I began a food blog that brought some purpose to my new life. I opened a small online shop, selling vintage and antique items that we found while visiting weekend markets called *brocantes*. Having an online shop opened up new styling and photography opportunities for me. I even shot food images for a local restaurant owner, who was self-publishing a *carnet de recettes*, a recipe booklet.

In early 2013, after more than two years of doing our best to make our little rental work, we felt the walls closing in, and our unhappiness growing. The house just didn't seem like us, and it didn't feel like home. At the time, there were also several other worrying events happening. My immigration status was turning out to be much less straightforward than we had thought it would be, and we deeply missed our friends and family back in the United States.

One morning, as I walked along the beach near our house, feeling certain I was the only one around for miles, I looked out at the horizon and up in the clouds and I had a conversation with God. Maybe I was pleading or perhaps negotiating and I wrapped up my rant by saying, "anything!" I will handle anything that comes my way with the grace I have never shown before, but I ask one thing: "I want a HOUSE—any house, big or small, anywhere. I want a house. We need a home!"

A week later, an ad popped up on my husband's computer screen, and he pointed it out to me. Pictured was a large brick-and-stone house, right off the autoroute in a town about twenty minutes away from where we were temporarily living since our arrival. It looked to be on abandoned farmland, overrun by wild rabbits. When we drove up the driveway a few days later to meet with the property agent, I didn't even need to go inside . . . Rabbit Hill, as we lovingly renamed it for our family, even in its state of semiabandon and disrepair, seemed perfect to us. We moved in that spring.

While waiting for our move-in day, we drove to the house regularly, took walks on the land in the snow, peeked into the windows, and started to brainstorm about our new life there. We marveled at the large empty spaces and tall ceilings. We made excuses for wobbly stairs and broken tiles. We passed the house at night, checking to see if the lights on the road would be too bright, and we counted hundreds and hundreds of rabbit families crossing the driveway in our headlights. Move-in day couldn't come soon enough.

For the first time in my life, I got to build a kitchen from scratch. Starting with nothing more than the electrical and plumbing in place, typical of an old French home, we put in furnishings, appliances, and storage. This room became the heart of the home and filled the rest of the house with contentment and purpose. Within the first year, we received six chickens from my husband's cousin, the first step toward making Rabbit Hill into Rabbit Hill farm. Eventually, we would add goats, sheep, ducks, geese, and two donkeys to that family of chickens.

I slowly became attuned to the changes in the produce and goods at the daily markets. I remember asking for celery in the summer, and the kind but firm way I was told that celery was available only in fall and winter. Market-to-table meant choosing what was currently grown or foraged for: asparagus in the spring, mushrooms in the fall, and endives in the winter. I became a student of the seasons, toting home newly discovered vegetables and ingredients and stepping outside of my culinary comfort zone.

But seasons are even more than that, and my seasons in France commenced when we landed in 2010, first living with my in-laws, then finding our first place, the arrival of our daughter, and the constant struggle to sort out the language and culture and find acceptance in a very established French family. Our seasons were filled with discovery, adjustment, resilience, celebration, and grace.

There's a quote from the movie *No Reservations* that has stuck with me: "I wish there was a cookbook for life . . . . Recipes telling us exactly what to do." Since arriving in France in 2010, food and cooking for the people I love have become the essentials of my cookbook for life.

Welcome to my home and to my kitchen at Rabbit Hill.

FRENCH KITCHEN TOOLS & UTENSILS

A Cook's *Batterie de Cuisine*

THERE ARE A FEW REASONS TO HAVE certain tools and utensils in your kitchen. The most obvious is that you should have all you need to execute a recipe with expertise and ease, but a second one might be that tools can become familiar friends on your cooking journey. A simple wooden spoon, for example. It is one of the most primitive utensils; the first evidence of its use dates back thousands of years. And yet, wooden spoons still take a place of honor next to modern materials like stainless steel and silicon. They will follow you from move to move and kitchen to kitchen. When packing a carton and heading to a new home, a box will surely be labeled in large permanent ink letters: wooden spoons and utensils—KITCHEN or OPEN FIRST.

When I travel, I always seek out a kitchen shop to purchase a wooden spoon from each location I visit or to commemorate a trip. Short- and long-handled wooden utensils sit in a place of honor in a large pottery crock on my counter, every single one of them getting regular use. I have a few special ones, a dark rustic wooden spoon that a friend sent me from the West Indies when she was in the Peace Corps (she and I had been apart for too long) and a beautifully hand-carved, long-handled risotto spoon, given to me by a new friend, who learned that I made risotto almost every Saturday night. These spoons all get better with age, smoothed by my hand, rounded and worn, some even bearing the telltale sign of a handle that got too close to the flames.

I have a 19th-century printers cabinet with stacks of slender drawers from back in the day of letterpresses and early publications. With some of the dividers removed, it is the perfect storage place for utensils and kitchen tools. The cabinet even has a slanted top, where open cookbooks can easily rest. It also houses my extensive collection of culinary knives, and I like to keep the drawer trays slightly open an inch or two so that the handles peek out to remind me how they are stored, and finding my favorites can be done with ease.

Knives are part of a cook's essential tools, and it is only in recent years that I came to understand all the different types and their uses. My knife skills are not at pro-level, but having a collection of sharp knives for designated tasks makes such a difference in everything I make. Don't undervalue the importance of smooth and uniform cuts, even if you aren't at the level of doing *tournée*, or julienne. To establish a set of most-used basics, I recommend a standard chef knife, a smaller utility knife, a paring knife, a serrated tomato knife, and a carving knife. As an extra, and a knife that is found in every French home, is a baguette or bread knife. When I travel, these knives are the ones I fold into my knife roll and tuck into my checked luggage so that even if I don't know what the kitchen I'll be working in might provide, my cutting needs are covered.

To round out my list of utensil essentials, I find placing multiple tongs near the stovetop are key, and mine hang with spatulas and small strainers, spoons, and small whisks. On the counter, a pottery crock holds antique table utensils, with bent fork tines and scratched spoons—aged and loved with a patina that shows steadfast lifelong use.

And finally, the heavy hitters in my kitchen are the cookware. Although I am most known for my love of copper cookware, thanks to my father-in-law and our mutual passion for restoring antique pieces, I still solidly believe that there are various types of cookware beyond copper that every kitchen needs. Whether copper or steel or iron, a good variety of saucepots—a tall, large-capacity stockpot and smaller ones for cooking pasta—and a few specialty pieces will complete your kitchen. And in every category of cookware, there are characteristics and details that make for significant differences. Thick walls and heavy bottoms are required for slow cooking and uniform heating and retention of temperature. Ovenproof handles and covers are essential for sauté pans so that they can be transferred from the stovetop to the oven. Cast iron can be heated to higher temperatures than any other cookware. Although it might seem like insignificant differences, I try to note these cookware specifics in my recipes.

In specialty cookware, I have a copper and porcelain double boiler or bain-marie that I never thought I would use. I was wrong, and it sits on my stovetop where I use it to slowly warm sauces, melt chocolate, and create custards. I also have an oddly shaped covered pot on my stovetop that was made solely for steaming potatoes and is aptly called a *pomme vapeur*. If you ever use one, you will know why it is so desired and often hard to come by.

In my collection of pots and pans, a Dutch oven tops the list of essentials. Although Dutch ovens are available in stainless steel, modern nonstick coatings, and other materials, I think that nothing is superior for slow cooking than enameled cast-iron (see more about Dutch ovens on page 170). In this book, I often use the term heavy-bottomed, which means that the base of the pot is made thicker than its walls. This heavy bottom aids in more even and moderate heating and a greater retention of heat at lower temperatures. The bonus is that cast-iron is almost indestructible, even in high-heat conditions, so it's also perfect for searing.

I have a slightly dented and lovely copper gratin pan that rarely returns to the pot rack. I use it for everything from *pommes frites*, or french fries, to quiches and frittatas, from gratins of vegetables to broiling pieces of fish. It doubles as a petite roasting pan when needed for cooking small chickens and roasts, and it is deep enough for making just the right amount of pan sauce. Other oven-to-table options include sturdy ironstone porcelain and pottery ovenware.

Slightly fancier but justifiable for those who love convenience are a mandoline (watch your fingertips and always use the guard!), poultry shears to cut through those bones for stock, and small appliances like a spice grinder (one that can handle both dry and wet ingredients). Rounding off my list of favorites is a high-quality immersion blender. In larger appliances, I have never regretted the investment of a good stand mixer.

IN MY OPINION, technique is far more important than recipes. Recipes may not stick in your mind, and that's why we bookmark and keep files and favorites, even after making a dish several times. But techniques—the methods to which most food is treated and prepared to its very best potential—once mastered, stay with you permanently.

Below is a basic glossary of a few of the most common techniques.

Blanching: Blanching is a cooking process in which food, usually a vegetable or a fruit, is scalded in boiling water, removed after a brief, timed interval, and finally plunged into ice water or placed under cold running water to halt the cooking process. This method makes vegetables like asparagus, green beans, and snap peas tender, allows them to retain their brilliant color, and ensures that they are perfectly cooked with just the right amount of crunch. Blanching can be used when you want to prep a vegetable for a cold dish or a salad. (**Tip:** Blanching is also the method used to easily remove the skins from tomatoes.)

Emulsifying: To emulsify means to combine two ingredients that do not ordinarily mix easily. The ingredients are usually a fat, like olive oil, and a water-based liquid, like broth, vinegar, or water itself. Emulsifying is what is needed to make a thick and creamy dressing, and it's a crucial step for making mayonnaise that is not running off the plate. (**Tip:** The trick to achieving emulsification is to use the correct proportions. The variables are the type of oil, the amount you use, the proportions of the thinner additions, such as lemon juice or water, and even the temperature of the ingredients.) In the end, let your eyes tell you when you are almost there and don't rush to add more oil or liquid. A tried-and-true method to get just the right amount of oil is to use a squeeze bottle and slowly add the oil in small amounts while rapidly whisking.

Poaching: Contrary to the image that poaching may conjure in your mind—a deep Jacuzzi-like pot of rapidly boiling liquid into which food is plopped to have a quick boil—poaching is actually a gentle and slow method that, when done attentively, produces the most delicious moist food product (or that perfect runny thick yolk!). To perfect your poaching technique, bring the water to just below boiling and gently submerge the food you wish to cook. Don't let the liquid come to a rolling boil; otherwise, your protein will be hard and overcooked, yet undercooked on the inside. When I poach chicken breast, for example, I slide the chicken into seasoned stock or liquid that has a few onions, celery, and carrots in it, poach it gently, check the internal temperature, and then remove it from the cooking liquid right away. (**Tip:** You can use the liquid to make a delicious sauce, such as Velouté (page 25).) I often make chicken this way in the summer and then chill it to have with a salad or homemade mayonnaise.

Searing: Before searing, dry the meat because, simply stated, you can't sear something that is wet. Follow these essentials for searing: Dry all meat, poultry, and even fish. Always use a very hot pan—smoking hot. Rub the meat (not the pan) with oil. Sear one side, sear the other side—REST. Let the meat rest, not you. But it is a good time to pour that glass of wine while you set up your pan sauce! (**Tip:** Searing is best done in a moderately heavy sauté pan. It is difficult to achieve a good sear in a pan with a nonstick surface, so just be aware.)

When searing meat for stew, dusting it with a little flour will enhance the formation of a golden "crust"; this also helps seal in the juices of the meat while it cooks. Simply lay the pieces of meat, after drying, on a platter or tray and then, using a fine-mesh colander, sprinkle the meat to evenly coat the pieces. I use a seasoned mixture of flour with a teaspoon of salt and freshly ground black pepper added.

Tempering: Essential for preventing lumps and scrambling, when a raw egg is added to warm or hot ingredients, tempering will save a sauce or batter from becoming a gloppy mess. For example, a custard or a sauce that requires adding whisked eggs to hot cream can be made silky-smooth by first adding a very small amount (about a soup spoon) of hot milk or cream and "tempering" the egg mixture by warming it rather than by combining all at once and "cooking" it. Tempering only takes a little bit of practice and is worth it to prevent the need to skim or strain cooked eggy bits.

Beyond the basics, below are a few extra techniques that you might find valuable.

Clarifying salted butter: This is done to remove the milk proteins from the fat in butter and results in a cooking ingredient that has a higher smoke point (can be heated without burning). Begin with unsalted butter since salt will be intensified by the reduction. Cut the butter into small 1-inch / 2.5 cm cubes and melt gently over low heat, in a shallow pan. Patience is of the essence because you don't want to overheat the butter but rather encourage the separation, which will begin to look like a pale foam on the surface of the heated butter. Using a slotted spoon, skim this foam and any white parts from the butter fat. Once the butter is clear, or clarified, pour it into a container and it is ready to use. You can safely keep it in a covered container for up to three months in the pantry or up to a year in the fridge.

Deglazing and reduction: Flavorful pan sauces would not exist without these essential methods. Begin by searing meats in a hot pan (see page 17). If creating a meat-based sauce, remove the meat before adding aromatics and vegetables. Sweat the vegetables (warming to the point of tenderness without browning) and then add wine, stock, or water to deglaze. Turn up the heat to high and stir while scraping the bottom of the pan to release the browned bits. Once this is done, reduce the heat, add more liquid, and cook until the liquid is reduced by one-third to one-half to make a sauce.

Rendering duck fat: This method comes in handy when you want to have duck fat on hand for sautéing or for confit. (Confit is a method of gently cooking in fat or oil at a low temperature). This rendering method is also used for cooking duck breast and rendering the fat to create a delicious crispy skin. For duck breasts, score the skin of each breast, taking care not to cut through to the meat. Add the breasts to a cold pan and heat slowly on medium heat until the fat begins to accumulate in the pan and can be drained off. You will repeat this several times until the skin becomes golden and most of the liquid fat is rendered. If you are using skin that has already been removed to make fat for cooking, you will first want to chop it into small pieces. Add the skin to a cold pan. This is very important, since you do not want to sear the skin because that will lock in the fat. Set the pan on very low heat and cook the skin slowly. Be sure not to allow the fat or skin to sizzle or brown. The fat will slowly melt or render, and once the fat is released, remove the skin bits with a slotted spoon. If there are small particles, use a fine-mesh strainer to remove them before storing. Rendered fat can be stored in an airtight container in the refrigerator for several months; however, once opened, it should be used within a few weeks. The fat can be frozen and reserved for future use for up to a year.

Basic French Pastry— *Brisée, Sucrée, Sablée*

You might be surprised to learn that the average French home cook does not make pastry. I think it's safe to say that as a culture, the French leave the pastry making to the patisserie chefs. But if you want to create your own, here are the standard recipes for three main types most often called for in French baking.

Pâte Brisée and Pâte Sucrée

Pâte brisée is an all-purpose classic pastry that has more butter to flour ratio than a standard piecrust. Most often used for savory tarts and pies, it is one of the three most common French pastry crusts; the others being *sucrée* and *sablée*, used for sweet creations. For this recipe, you can use a food processor or work by hand, using a pastry cutter.

Pâte Sucrée — For sweet desserts and tarts, add 1½ teaspoons of sugar to the recipe below.

MAKES ONE 12-INCH OR 30 CM DIAMETER ROUND PASTRY

> ½ cup / 110 g chilled salted butter, cut into 1–inch / 2.5 cm pieces
>
> 1¼ cups / 150 g all-purpose flour, plus more for flouring surface
>
> 3 to 4 tablespoons / 45 to 60 ml ice water, plus more as needed

Cut the butter into small cubes. In a food processor, combine the flour with 4 tablespoons / 55 g of the butter, using the pulse setting on your food processor until the mixture resembles coarse sand. Add the remaining butter. The pieces of butter should be pea size. Slowly add the ice water in a steady stream, pulsing between additions.

Turn the dough mixture onto a lightly floured surface or onto parchment paper and knead with the heel of your hand until it comes together in one form. Do not overhandle, as the butter will become warm; you want the dough to stay as cold as possible.

Roughly flatten the dough into a disk. Cover in plastic wrap and chill for 2 hours.

The pastry can be wrapped tightly in plastic and frozen for up to a month and thawed in the refrigerator before use. When you are ready to use the pastry, let it sit at room temperature for 10 minutes. Roll out the pastry to form a 12-inch / 30 cm diameter round or to the size needed. The rolled dough should be about ⅛ inch / 3 mm in thickness.

Pâte Sablée

Pâte sablée is a short-crust pastry, specifically used for desserts. Its name comes from its slightly "sandy" texture that is due to the addition of almond flour. The finished crust is rolled thicker than standard pastry to make a substantial cookielike foundation for tarts and custard desserts.

MAKES 1 (8 TO 10-INCH / 20 TO 25 CM) ROUND PASTRY, OR ROUND TART CRUST

continues >

½ cup / 110 g cold butter

¾ cup / 150 g sugar

2 cups / 240 g all-purpose flour, plus more for flouring surface

⅓ cup / 30 g almond flour

1 large egg, lightly beaten

Cut the butter into small cubes.

In a small bowl, combine the sugar and all-purpose and almond flours. Add the butter and rub the mixture between your hands (or lightly pulse if using a food processor), until a sandy mixture is formed. Add the egg and mix until combined.

Knead the dough on a floured surface, until it begins to form a ball. If the dough becomes sticky, you can pop it back into the refrigerator to chill for 10 minutes before continuing. Roll out the pastry to a ¼-inch / 6 mm thickness or press it into a tart pan or pie dish.

getting the most from store-bought pastry

I think you can confidently bake with store-bought pastry with these few essential pointers.

INGREDIENTS: Top on the list of importance for good pastry are organic flour and pure butter. Many brands will sneak in processed lard or vegetable shortening or hydrogenated fats, which are processed fats that are high in trans fats and have been linked to heart disease and inflammation and have no nutritional value. There are so many additions to industrial or mass-produced pastry to color it, make it seem flakier, or add artificial flavor. *Non. Non. Non.* Put it back on the shelf!

FRESH OR FROZEN: Most often, store-bought pastry can be found in a store's freezer section and will need to thaw in the refrigerator for a minimum of 8 hours before use. Don't be tempted to leave it out on the counter to thaw, as the butter will soften and the resulting pastry will be flat and oily.

HOW TO USE: Cold butter in pastry is the key to light and flaky pastry so if you are rolling it out or cutting it into shapes, pop it back into the fridge for 15 minutes before you top or fill it. If you are rolling it into shape, use a lightly floured surface so you can easily move it from surface to pan or tart molds.

PREBAKING PASTRY: Sometimes called parbaking or blind baking, this is done when a pastry might absorb too much liquid from the filling or if the bake time is not sufficient to thoroughly bake the pastry bottom. Blind baking is done for pastry that needs to be baked entirely for a nonbaked filling, such as pudding or custard. Before baking, weigh down the piecrust with pie weights, dry beans, or rice so it doesn't puff up in the center or shrink down the sides. Carefully line the pie dough with parchment paper first, then add some weight. Parbaking normally takes 10 minutes or less, while blind baking will take 15 minutes or more.

TO WASH OR NOT? Everyone loves a golden crust, and it's up to the baker to determine whether to enhance the natural browning with an egg wash or milk. My standard for basic pastry is one yolk mixed with a drizzle of cold water, which I think gives consistent results and a lovely golden color.

A FINAL RULE OF THUMB: Follow the instructions on the package and use the guidelines for temperature and cook time.

ALTHOUGH THERE ARE countless sauces in French cuisine, most are derived from five mother sauces, specified by Chef Auguste Escoffier in the early 19th century. Each of the five is differentiated by its base or thickening agent. The five sauces are béchamel, velouté, espagnole, hollandaise, and tomate.

Despite what you might think, technique is more essential with sauces than measured ingredients, and the ability to improvise or to correct a sauce is key. Who hasn't had a failed cheese sauce or a broken hollandaise? It's not the kind of pressure we want to have riding on us when creating a meal. If the sauce is bad, there is too much at stake. I learned this when we had our bed and breakfast and were making eggs Benedict almost daily. No matter how perfectly poached the egg was or how crispy the croissant (which we subbed for the traditional English muffin), if the hollandaise was globby or oily or too thin . . . the entire dish lost its appeal.

If asked, I would say that my favorite sauce technique is a pan sauce, and that might sound surprising because that doesn't even make the list of classic French sauces. But my feeling is that a simple and delicious pan sauce can make a boring dish exceptional and an exceptional dish stunning. In our home, the common question every time I cook meats or poultry or even fish is, "Is there a sauce?" And if there is a sauce, and there always is . . . there must always be bread. And I think you know why.

A Few Notes About Ingredients

You will notice these consistencies throughout all the recipes. When butter is noted as an ingredient, I am most always suggesting *beurre demi-sel,* or salted butter. There are only very few exceptions, and for those, I note unsalted. Throughout my years of cooking, I have always preferred using salted butter rather than adding more salt to the recipe that calls for unsalted butter. Also, I use only pure butter not altered with any other ingredients. Clarified butter is also exceptional for cooking (see page 18), and when sautéing, adding a bit of olive oil (you will notice I often list these ingredients side by side) prevents butter from browning too quickly and enhances the butter flavor in the recipe.

Salt when specified in the recipes, is always sea salt, pure and noniodized. If finishing salt is noted, it is *fleur de sel* which is a hand-harvested sea salt found in coastal areas like Brittany and used specifically for finishing. Its fine crystals do not dissolve and are meant to accentuate flavor while adding the tiny crunch of salt.

For dairy products, I recommend only whole milk and full-fat creams. Using low-fat and skim milks, crème fraîche (sour cream), and yogurt will most likely separate or thin a sauce, so the recipe's desired result may not be achieved.

Béchamel Sauce

I would probably say that the most practical sauce to master is the béchamel sauce. This creamy white sauce that features milk over heavy cream is not only the base for a multitude of sauces but it's also essential for so many traditional French dishes, from cheese soufflés to vegetable dishes and gratins. I learned how to make a béchamel sauce as a young cook so I could make a super-creamy mac 'n' cheese and cheese sauces for broccoli and cauliflower. It is a basic and easy sauce with just a few ingredients.

The first thing I can tell you about this simple and practical sauce is that you always use exactly the same amount of butter and flour. Always. And once you've made this sauce a few times, you will get very good at eyeballing the amounts. After that, once you have your roux, a mixture of fat and flour, the rest is completely adjustable (and fixable if needed!).

This sauce is interesting because it does work with lower-fat milk, although I don't recommend it. But if that is all you have on hand, it can work in a pinch. In this situation, the butter can compensate for the fat removed from the milk, and the flour functions as a thickener and also a binder. In other French sauces, full-fat cream is a must so that the sauce stays intact and doesn't separate.

MAKES 2 CUPS / 480 ML

- 2 tablespoons salted butter
- 2 tablespoons all-purpose flour
- 2 cups / 480 ml whole milk, at room temperature
- Salt and freshly ground black pepper
- Pinch of nutmeg (optional)

In a small saucepan over low heat, melt the butter, then add the flour and increase the heat to medium. Heat the butter and flour until the flour "cooks." This is essential to prevent a raw flour taste. I use the smell test to determine when it has been heated sufficiently (it will smell toasty rather than floury), and often the flour–butter mixture will foam or bubble a little, signaling that it is time to add the milk.

It's best to use room temperature milk rather than cold to avoid lumps, and if you have a fast whisking hand, you can even add hot milk that will thicken almost immediately. Continuously whisk, until you are happy with the consistency. Don't worry if the sauce is too thin, continue to simmer and it will thicken gradually and continue even once off the heat.

Once the sauce starts to bubble, lower the heat and stir frequently. (This is the stage to add cheese or other additions, depending on the sauce you are making.) If just making a white sauce, add salt and pepper to taste and the nutmeg (if using). If you aren't using the sauce right away, you can put a small amount of butter on the surface to keep a skin from forming or whisk in a little more hot milk to smooth it out again.

VARIATIONS

Mornay Sauce

TO THE WARM BÉCHAMEL SAUCE BASE, ADD:

- 3 egg yolks
- 3½ tablespoons / 50 ml heavy cream
- 1 cup / 100 g finely grated Gruyère, Comté, or Emmentaler cheese
- Salt

In a bowl, mix together the egg yolks and cream. Slowly add the egg and cream mixture to the béchamel base and increase the heat while whisking. Once the sauce begins to bubble, add the grated cheese and combine until melted. Add salt to taste (will depend on the saltiness and flavor of the cheese that you are using).

Velouté Sauce

TO THE WARM BÉCHAMEL SAUCE BASE, ADD:

4 cups / 960 ml cold chicken, vegetable, or fish stock

Add the stock to the béchamel base and whisk to combine. Heat for 30 minutes on low or until the desired thickness is achieved.

Soubise Sauce

TO THE WARM BÉCHAMEL SAUCE BASE, ADD:

2 medium onions, finely sliced

3 ½ tablespoons / 50 g salted butter

5 tablespoons / 75 ml heavy cream

Salt and freshly ground black pepper

Sauté the onions in the butter until tender, about 15 minutes on low heat. Add the onions to the béchamel base and simmer for 10 minutes. If you prefer a smooth sauce, you can use an immersion blender to fully combine the onions in the sauce. Reheat the sauce and add the cream. Add salt and pepper to taste.

Tip: Be careful not to allow the sauce to come to a boil, which might cause the sauce to split. If this should happen, drizzle in a small amount of boiling water and whisk rapidly.

Hollandaise Sauce

Originally created in Normandy, hollandaise sauce was referred to as Sauce Isigny, prior to World War I. As Normandy made its mark as a region that produces some of the best butter and cream in France, the sauce became widely used. During and after the war, when dairy products were scarce, Dutch butter was imported for this use—hence the name change. Most likely, you have had hollandaise sauce many times. It's the standard sauce for eggs Benedict, many fish dishes, and as a sauce for asparagus. Although it is a basic sauce composed of egg yolks, butter, and acid (most commonly lemon juice but sometimes vinegar), it can be a tricky one to master. A good hollandaise sauce will be buttery, smooth, and slightly tangy. A bad one will be oily, salty, or overly lemony. I made hollandaise sauce almost every morning when we had a bed and breakfast, and once I learned that it could be "saved" using a few easy tips, it was far less daunting. Eventually, I didn't even need a recipe.

½ cup / 110 g unsalted butter or clarified butter (see page 18)

1 tablespoon lemon juice

3 egg yolks, at room temperature, lightly beaten

1 teaspoon Dijon mustard (optional)

Salt and freshly ground black pepper to taste

Begin by whisking the egg yolks with the lemon juice and set aside. Melt the butter using a double boiler or a bain-marie (a glass bowl over a pot of boiling water).

Once the butter is melted, turn off the heat and temper the eggs with a few spoons of the warm butter (as described on page 18). Repeat until the eggs and butter are about the same temperature and then whisk the egg and lemon juice mixture into the remaining salted butter. Turn the heat under the double boiler back to a low simmer and whisk the sauce to thicken. Add the mustard as a final step and add salt and pepper to taste.

notes

If the sauce overthickens, remove the pan from the heat and whisk in a drizzle of boiling water. You can also save a thick or lumpy sauce by whisking in a few tablespoons of warm cream. This method also works if the sauce sits and becomes solid or if the fat of the butter "splits" from the eggs.

Basic Mayonnaise

Similar to hollandaise sauce but technically not a sauce, mayonnaise is essential in many French recipes. It's worth mastering it if only to avoid those extra unneeded ingredients in processed mass-produced condiments. It's also a great way to feature free-range farm eggs and their brilliantly orange yolks. Here are a few important tips: (1) Make sure all the ingredients are at room temperature, especially the yolks. Julia Child recommends warming a glass or pottery bowl before you begin. (2) You can whisk by hand or use a food processor or immersion blender. I find with an electric blender or beater that you have less control of the emulsion, but if you feel confident in the process, then it does save time. (3) I also recommend working in single batches, since when making a larger amount, it becomes harder to get the perfect consistency. (4) Finally, to regulate the amount of oil added, fill a squeeze bottle with the oil; this will allow you to add the oil in a slow, perfect drizzle or only a few drops at a time.

MAKES ABOUT 1 CUP / 240 G

- 2 large egg yolks
- 1 teaspoon Dijon mustard
- 1 tablespoon lemon juice
- 1 cup / 240 ml canola or peanut oil
- Sea salt

In a glass bowl, add the egg yolks and mustard and whisk until well incorporated and evenly thick. Add the lemon juice and whisk for 30 seconds. Very slowly drizzle in the oil, while rapidly whisking to emulsify. Check consistency and stop once the mayonnaise is at your desired thickness (you might not use all the oil) before adding the salt. If by chance the mayonnaise is overbeaten and curdles, you can add a tiny amount of very hot water and whisk.

Store the mayonnaise in an airtight container in the refrigerator for up to 3 days.

Classic French Vinaigrette

I would be remiss not to add a recipe for the classic vinaigrette. It's the standard dressing for most green salads served both at home and when eating out. Occasionally, it will have a slight variation, perhaps with the addition of fresh herbs or a touch of honey, but otherwise the basic recipe has remained the same for centuries. Most often, this dressing is prepared in the bottom of a large bowl and then the washed and dried greens are placed on top and only tossed once at the table. In France, making a vinaigrette is almost always done by eye and taste, and ingredients are rarely measured. Once you have made it a few times, you will adjust it by habit. I like mine a touch more acidic and add more vinegar, while my husband likes his a bit more mustardy. Balsamic or apple cider vinegar work as well.

MAKES ½ CUP / 120 ML

- 2 tablespoons finely chopped shallots
- 2 tablespoons red or white wine vinegar
- 2 teaspoons Dijon mustard
- 4 to 6 tablespoons / 60 to 90 ml olive oil
- Salt and freshly ground black pepper

In a large bowl, combine the shallots and vinegar and then mix with the mustard. Slowly drizzle in the oil and rapidly whisk until emulsified. Add salt and pepper to taste.

Store the dressing in an airtight container at room temperature for up to 1 week or in the refrigerator almost indefinitely.

IT DIDN'T TAKE LONG for me to realize that those convenient boxes of stock (formerly produced in cans) were not commonly available in France. I must say that we were completely spoiled when we lived in the United States and could easily acquire high-quality organic stocks from the local grocery store (and at all hours of the day). Searching the aisles at even the largest supermarkets in France did not yield a single carton, and I soon learned that if stock was required for a recipe or soup, there were two options: bouillon cubes or make your own.

That said, I think there are many times when a store-bought stock is perfectly fine, especially with the range and quality of products that are available. There are only a few that I feel aren't comparable or should not be purchased premade; one is fish stock. I think it is difficult to get the flavor just right and the vibrancy of fresh fish stock is lost in the carton versions. I also believe that with top-quality bouillon cubes (organic, less salt, and so on), you can make most vegetable soups and not tell the difference. Cubes also work well when you need only a cup or less of bouillon for a sauce or for deglazing.

On the opposite end are the stocks and broths that can make or break a dish. And for those times, you will want to have homemade stock ready to go. The good news is that stocks can be made in very large batches with no difference in effort and freeze perfectly in airtight containers or resealable bags.

Making Stock

In my kitchen, there are a few set "rules" around making stock that are a result of perfecting it over the past ten years. Here are some things you can do to make a stock that excels in both flavor and nutrition. It takes only a few extra steps that are well worth the effort.

INGREDIENTS

Always start with the best (organic, local, and fresh) ingredients. When you make stock, you are in essence concentrating every part of the meat, bone, and vegetables to extract flavor. But you are also extracting anything that was used to grow the vegetable or raise the meat, so in terms of industrial meat and poultry, or nonorganic produce, why would you want to concentrate that?

METHOD

There is a French method of making stock that entails browning the ingredients to make a "golden" stock. Once I tried this method, I never wanted to go back to any other practice. I just don't believe, and I think this technique proves, that flavorful stock can be achieved by a whole raw chicken and vegetables submerged in water, even when cooked for hours and hours. The technique I recommend and stand by is to first brown the poultry or meat (and even marrow bones if making bone broth), then adding the vegetables to also "sweat" or begin to release their natural juices, and finally, adding a few cloves of garlic and sautéing until golden—before adding any water or other seasoning.

ENHANCING THE STOCK

The bone broth trend has hit its height over the past decade. Bones themselves are rich in vitamins and nutrients, including calcium, magnesium, and phosphorus. Nutritionists and scientists claim that the natural collagen in broth from bone acts as an anti-inflammatory, aids in boosting immunity, and is also thought to promote joint health. No wonder cooks make chicken soup when feeling a cold or flu coming on!

But how do you get the most benefit from bones in stock? The amount of collagen in bones varies. Fish and pork have very high levels and hence make a thick gelatinous stock. Duck bones, which are very dense (and hard to chop through!), release a higher amount of collagen than other poultry. Beef bones, with their large ratio of marrow, are high in nutrients like vitamin A and K, zinc, and iron. But dropping bones into a pot of water or broth is not enough to get all that goodness. Adding 2 tablespoons of apple cider vinegar to the stockpot not only makes the bones more porous but also releases more collagen and nutrients. Whether using leftover bones from a roast chicken or fresh chicken parts, chop each bone in half between the joints with a cleaver or poultry shears to release even more of the collagen while cooking.

For both flavor and health benefits, add turmeric to your stock. A teaspoon of powder or a thumb-size piece of root cut into halves adds both flavor, anti-inflammatory attributes, and that gorgeous golden color. Be sure to add whole peppercorns, too. Just a tablespoon will not make the stock peppery but will help your body absorb the turmeric. And finally, add a couple of whole "bruised" or torn bay leaves, which add a lovely taste and also have antiviral properties.

I don't reserve this method for just sipping stock, as we call it, although we love having a few liters to heat up by the cupful all day long during the winter months. Preparing the stock in this way makes the most flavorful and richest stock for all your soup and sauce needs!

Golden Chicken Broth

In the cooler months, I make at least one batch of broth per week. It is quickly used or enjoyed and, on a rare occasion, there might be a little left to store in the freezer. I think fresh raw chicken and poultry make the best stock, but it is perfectly fine to jump a few steps ahead if you are using bones from a previously cooked chicken. Just be sure that you still chop the bones open so they release the maximum amount of collagen while cooking. This same method works for all poultry, including duck, turkey, and goose. There are two methods that differ only in whether you want to save the meat for other uses or leave it for the full cooking time. I share both below.

MAKES 8 CUPS / 1.9 L

> 3 tablespoons / 45 ml olive oil
>
> 4 pounds / 1.75 kg chicken legs and thighs
>
> 1 medium onion, quartered
>
> 1 large carrot, coarsely chopped
>
> 1 large celery stalk, cut into 4 pieces
>
> 2 garlic cloves, halved
>
> 2 tablespoons apple cider vinegar
>
> 1 teaspoon coarse salt
>
> ½ tablespoon whole peppercorns
>
> 1 thumb-size turmeric root (optional)
>
> 1 bay leaf
>
> 8 cups / 2 L cold water

In a large soup pot over medium-high heat, heat the oil and brown the chicken on all sides.

Add the onion, carrot, celery, and garlic and cook for about 5 minutes. Add the vinegar, salt, peppercorns, turmeric, and bay leaf. Add the water and cover.

Cook the stock for 5 to 8 hours at a low simmer. If using the meat from the chicken parts, remove the meat from the bones after about 90 minutes. Leaving it longer will make it flavorless and stringy in texture. Add the bones back into the stock and continue to simmer for the remaining time. Chop the chicken meat and store it in the refrigerator for other uses.

When the stock has finished cooking, strain the vegetables and bones and let the stock cool for about 20 minutes before putting it into the refrigerator.

Store the stock in an airtight container in the refrigerator for up to 5 days or freeze for up to 6 months.

tip

Remember to pat the chicken dry so the skin can brown nicely; this adds rich flavor and color to the broth. You can do this by drying the chicken parts with a paper towel or kitchen towel before adding to the pan.

Mirepoix is a term that describes a set ratio of three standard ingredients: celery, onion, and carrots. The word is derived from the name of a medieval town and an 18th-century duke who resided there as a chef de cuisine and who standardized the use of this exact combination of vegetables in preparation of classic dishes. The French mirepoix consists of finely chopped quantities of one part celery to two parts onions and one part carrots. Commonly sautéed in butter, oil, or fat, this is a standard base for almost all stews, soups, and many sauces. When I am setting up my mise en place, I always begin with chopping and arranging the bowls of my mirepoix first.

Flavorful Fish Stock

Fish stock is an essential base for many seafood dishes and sauces, and store-bought ones are rarely up to par. I like to make a large batch and freeze the rest for later use in soups or sauces. Sometimes, you can get the bones, heads, and parts of fish for free from your fishmonger; just be sure to avoid using the bones of oily fish, such as salmon, mackerel, or tuna, since they are too fatty and will make your stock greasy. Be careful when seasoning fish stock. If you intend to reduce it for a sauce, do not add any salt until right at the end, since the saltiness will intensify as the stock cooks and can become overpowering. Many bouillon cubes for stock have excess salt added, so be sure to use a high-quality one and monitor the saltiness before seasoning.

MAKES ABOUT 4 CUPS / 960 ML

> 1 or 2 medium whole fish, approximately 3 pounds / 1½ kg, cleaned, scaled, and rinsed
>
> 2 carrots, halved
>
> 2 celery stalks with leaves, halved or quartered
>
> 1 onion, halved
>
> 6 cups / 1.5 L cold water
>
> A few sprigs of fresh thyme
>
> 1 bay leaf
>
> 2 cubes vegetable bouillon (optional, but adds to the flavor)
>
> Salt (optional)

Set a stockpot over high heat and add the fish, carrots, celery, and onion. Cover with cold water and bring to a boil.

Turn down the heat to low and add the thyme, bay leaf, and bouillon cubes, then simmer for an hour until the fish breaks down. Taste and add a bit of salt as needed.

continues >

Remove the pot from the heat and set aside to cool. Place a fine-mesh strainer over a large bowl and strain the liquid, discarding the solids.

Stock can be stored in the refrigerator in a sealed jar for up to 3 days. Fish stock freezes beautifully if your recipe calls for only a cup or two and can be frozen in batches for up to 6 months.

Rich Beef Stock

In France, I use what is called pot-au-feu beef along with several marrow bone sections to make stock, but any bone-in cut will work. We love keeping the broth in the refrigerator to heat up and drink like tea in the cold months. Of course, beef stock is also the star ingredient for Soupe à l'Oignon (page 51), and it freezes well to keep on hand for sauces. Roasting the bones and vegetables as a first step imparts a slightly smoky flavor to the broth.

MAKES 5 QUARTS / APPROXIMATELY 4.75 L

Olive oil for drizzling

8 beef marrow bones

4 pounds / 1.75 kg bone-in beef, such as shank, shoulder, or oxtail

3 medium onions, skins on, halved

4 carrots, chopped

1 small head of garlic (4 or 5 cloves)

4 celery stalks, chopped

½ teaspoon sea salt

½ tablespoon whole peppercorns

5 quarts / 4.75 L cold water

2 bay leaves

¼ cup / 60 ml apple cider vinegar

Preheat the oven to 450°F / 230°C. Drizzle a sheet pan with the oil.

Lay the marrow bones and beef scraps on the prepared pan. Place the onions, cut side down, on the pan, then add the carrots.

Cut the garlic one-quarter from the end to reveal the cloves but so it still holds together. Lay the garlic face down on the pan. Place the pan in the oven and roast the bones and vegetables for 25 minutes.

Remove the pan from the oven and scrape the beef and vegetables into a large soup pot. Add the celery, salt, and peppercorns. Add the water, bay leaves, and vinegar.

Set the pot over high heat and bring the stock to a full boil, then turn down the heat, cover, and simmer for 6 to 8 hours. It will be good at 6 hours, but better after 8. Pour the stock through a fine-mesh strainer, then discard the beef and vegetables. Set the stock aside to cool.

Store the stock in an airtight container in the refrigerator for 1 week, or in the freezer for up to 6 months.

Savory Ham Stock

I love making ham stock to use in split pea or bean soups. Its inherently subtle smokiness and high amount of natural collagen make it an exceptional choice for that perfect extra layer of *fumé* flavor. The stock does need a slight boost of seasoning, and this can be achieved by adding a couple of high-quality vegetable bouillon cubes. I reserve ham bones in the freezer, until I have collected enough to make a large pot of stock. Once made, the stock freezes beautifully.

MAKES 4¼ QUARTS / 4 L

continues >

1 tablespoon olive oil

2 medium onions, skins on, halved

4 carrots, chopped

4 celery stalks, chopped

2 garlic cloves, halved

2 to 4 large ham bones

5 quarts / 4.75 L cold water

¼ cup / 60 ml apple cider vinegar

2 vegetable bouillon cubes

½ tablespoon whole peppercorns

1 bay leaf

In a large soup pot over high heat, warm the oil. Add the onion, carrots, celery, and garlic, then turn down the heat to medium and cook for 5 minutes, until vegetables take on a little color.

Add the ham bones and water, return the heat to high, and add the vinegar, bouillon, and peppercorns. Break the bay leaf in half and add it to the pot. Once the stock starts to boil, turn down the heat to low, and let the stock simmer continuously for 3 hours; do not let the stock boil.

Pour the stock through a fine-mesh strainer, then discard the ham and vegetables. Set the stock aside to cool.

Store the stock in quart- or liter-size glass jars in the refrigerator for up to 5 days or the freezer for up to 6 months. Leave ½ inch / 1.5 cm of headspace for expansion if freezing.

mise en place

Mise en place is a French culinary phrase which means "everything in its place." It refers to the preparation and setup that a cook does prior to creating a dish. It is the cook's palette, so to speak, and in my mind, it promotes ease and creativity in the kitchen.

In the home kitchen, it allows you to focus on just the basic ingredients and have everything set and arranged; the extra bonus is that cleanup becomes so much easier since food items are back in the pantry or fridge before you even start cooking. In professional kitchens, it is one of the first things a sous chef is taught and it promotes the precision and organization that is required by a chef. An easy way to make this technique of precooking prep a habit is to set small bowls out on your counter (equal or similar size) and then handle the ingredients one at a time, cutting and measuring each as specified in the recipe. You can even line up each bowl in the order of which they will be used. This way, once you start to cook, you are never turning your back on a pan on the heat or on a tempering sauce.

Lots of good things happen in a kitchen when things are organized and ready! Conversations while cooking take place without distraction or detriment to the process. And it's easy to enlist guests to help, (because they will always ask if there is anything they can do!) if you have multiple small bowls of ingredients ready to go ahead of time. There is also intention and a kind of reverence given to each and every ingredient. And if you are creating your own recipe or your take on a recipe, you can easily make notes on additions and tweaks by visually seeing everything laid out. It helps new cooks feel in control by anticipating what is needed for a dish.

On the topic of measurements, I normally cook by sight and instinct—except when baking, which needs to be somewhat precise. Although I encourage you to do the same, measurements do help when learning a dish for the first time. I also cook with metric measurements and by weight versus volume when it comes to dry ingredients, but I have converted most ingredients for American cooks in order to make the ingredients lists and preparation as clear as possible. There isn't a direct conversion from metric to imperial units, or an exact conversion table, but in most cases, I think a rough conversion will work. I have even found that by preparing your *mise en place* as a habit, you become better and better at visually estimating your ingredient measurements and quantities.

The goal is to feel comfortable while you cook. The more you cook and try new recipes, the better you will become at estimating or cooking by intuition. You will also develop your personal taste and learn the tastes of the people you are cooking for, which will allow you to get creative and confident and have more fun in the kitchen—the ultimate goal!

SPRING
LE PRINTEMPS

SPRING ON THE FARM is full of anticipation. We search for tiny sprouts and signs of life and our minds are filled with early planning, seed ordering, and weekend cleanup of the potager gardens.

Daffodils, our lovely, wild, early spring warriors, surprised us in our first months on the farm, arriving even before the first official day of the season. Planted perhaps many decades ago, the bulbs are hidden away on the hilly sides of a little natural creek. Despite sometimes being trampled by cows, or fully flooded in torrential winter downpours, they come up, year after year. We make our way through the muddy pathways to check on them, and once they appear, we cut dozens of stalks to fill glass jars in the kitchen and bring to friends.

Beyond that, the farm is quiet in spring. During the periods when we bred the goats, the kids would arrive in March or April, and in some years, when we were not certain exactly when the goats might have had a "date" with our buck, we would begin the watch in February, checking udders and watching for slightly quirky behaviors and signals that things would be moving along.

Our last season of breeding was in 2020, and we had a surprising season of nine births that year, including a set of triplets. Many a late night or early morning was spent in the goat room of the barn, where we learned more that season about goats and kids than we learned in all of the years before and since.

The chickens and ducks return to work in the spring, providing more eggs than we can consume. The geese, who produce forty eggs each twice a year, provide huge thick-shelled eggs that can singly make a family omelet or soufflé for six.

We begin to look for the first harvests of asparagus and spring greens at our market, and Easter menu ideas start to unfold in my mind. In a way, we come out of hibernation, our palettes ready for fresh textures and flavors, as days become longer and we relish the brighter sunny skies.

cooking french

After only a couple of years, my kitchen was buzzing at Rabbit Hill. My love for sharing recipes was ignited by making connections with those who adored my Friday evening social media posts and the very popular Slow Cooking Sunday editions on Instagram. Since we had been hosting meals and gatherings in association with providing vintage shopping tours, opening our kitchen was a natural progression, and teaching French cooking and techniques became a steadfast passion. Inspired by my father-in-law and other professional chefs, the places where we had eaten, and the books I had read, we loved being able to share everything we had learned with visitors.

Soon, our home was filled with guests from all over the world, eager to experience daily French life, going with us to the market, and preparing a French feast. From classic bistro food to fancy formal dishes, menus were created based on the desires and curiosity of the guests; what they wanted to eat and what they wanted to master. Once or twice a month, guests would crowd into the kitchen and fill the dining table, and we would create five-course menus that highlighted seasonal dishes and local ingredients. And even more than a full house or a busy kitchen, having this opportunity also filled our hearts.

Each workshop guest received an apron, a notebook, and a pen and was encouraged to take on preparation tasks and learn techniques. Our goal always was to make each of them feel welcome, no matter their cooking level, and to teach in a way that allowed them to return home feeling inspired and confident.

Over the years, we have been blessed to meet some very special people. Over plates of delicious food, full glasses of wine (and maybe a shot or two of Calvados!), we have laughed, cried, and been reminded that it's not just the food, the rooms we gather in, or even a beautiful kitchen that inspires or heals us but the connections that are made in a safe, homey space with a table lit with candles signifying warmth and light that says, "Welcome, we are glad you are here."

The meals we have shared with people who might otherwise not have passed through our lives will forever be, to me, one of the most priceless opportunities I have had. Sharing, encouraging, empowering through teaching . . . all are lessons of grace that remain long after the apron has been hung up and the candles extinguished.

Gougères

A *gougère* is a baked savory pastry made of choux dough mixed with cheese. The first time I had *gougères* was at a bistro in Paris, and they were served to us while we perused the menu. Served on a small porcelain saucer, there were four of them for the two of us, and after the first bite, I knew I would have to have more. There are many variations, but the cheeses that are most commonly used are grated Gruyère, Comté, and Emmentaler.

MAKES 12 PASTRIES

1 cup / 240 ml water

5½ tablespoons / 80 g unsalted butter, cut into ½-inch / 1.5 cm cubes

1 cup / 120 g all-purpose flour

¾ teaspoon salt

Pinch of freshly ground black pepper

4 large eggs

2 cups / 200 g grated Comté cheese, with a few tablespoons reserved for topping

1 large egg yolk, beaten, for brushing

Poppy seeds, for topping

Preheat the oven to 425°F / 220°C. Line a baking sheet with parchment paper.

In a saucepan over medium-high heat, combine the water and butter. Bring to a boil until the butter is melted. Remove the pan from the stove, then add the flour, salt, and pepper and mix until incorporated.

Return the pan to the stove over low heat and mix for 1 minute. Remove the pan from the stove and let sit for 2 minutes. Add 1 of the eggs and mix vigorously until incorporated; at first, the mixture will look quite gloppy, but the more you beat it, the smoother and stickier it will become. Add the 3 remaining eggs, one at a time, mixing until incorporated before adding the next. By this time, your arm might be getting a bit achy, but persevere! Then, stir in the cheese.

Drop 1 tablespoon mounds or fill a piping bag and place one small dollop onto the prepared baking sheet about 3 inches / 7.5 cm apart. Brush lightly with the egg yolk (when I pipe, I do not do this, since it flattens the design), then top with a pinch of the reserved cheese and poppy seeds.

Bake for 25 minutes. Remove the baking sheet from the oven and place on a wire rack to cool for 15 minutes so the *gougères* become crispy on the exterior and the inside dries slightly. Serve warm or at room temperature.

You can bake these one day ahead and place in a 350°F / 180°C oven for 15 minutes to crisp up before serving.

Oeufs Mayonnaise

Hardboiled Eggs and Homemade Mayonnaise

I must admit my surprise the first time I saw such a simple dish on a Paris bistro menu. A friend ordered it, and it was a basic plating of a hard-boiled egg with mayonnaise and sliced red tomatoes. This version adds a bit of fancy to a long-standing traditional bistro appetizer and uses what a restaurant would call mayonnaise *fait maison*, or "homemade." The presentation is done with a fresh tomato salad and mixed spring herbs.

SERVES 4

4 large eggs

1 small heirloom tomato, thinly sliced

2 teaspoons olive oil

Fleur de sel, for sprinkling the tomatoes

2 tablespoons Basic Mayonnaise (page 26), plus more for plating

Assortment of fresh herbs, such as chives, flat-leaf parsley, or dill, for garnish

Set a large pot of water over high heat and bring to a boil. Add the eggs and boil, uncovered, for 9 minutes. Remove the eggs from the pot and allow to cool on a plate or kitchen towel.

Place the tomatoes on a plate and drizzle with the oil, then sprinkle with the fleur de sel.

Peel the eggs, cut each end to make a flat bottom, then slice in half to make "bowls." Remove the yolks and combine with a few spoonfuls of mayonnaise. Fill a piping bag with the yolk filling and fill the egg bowls or fill them using a small spoon.

Spread several spoonfuls of mayonnaise onto each plate and place the eggs on top. Serve with the tomato slices and a garnish of fresh herbs.

Pâté de Campagne — Country-Style Pâté

Pâté de campagne, or "country pâté," is frequently served as a starter in classic French bistros, along with a basket of bread and an aperitif drink. Made in a porcelain or pottery mold, it cooks for several hours and is then served cold in slices alongside a bowl of cornichons, which are tiny little pickles brined in vinegar with herbs, and occasionally with mustard. Fatty pork shoulder (about 20 percent fat) and pork belly work best for this recipe, and I have substituted a small amount of duck fat instead of the foie gras (duck or goose liver) normally called for. I grind the pork using the grinder attachment on my stand mixer, but in a pinch, you can use a food processor. You can also have your butcher grind the meat in advance.

SERVES 4 TO 6 PEOPLE AS AN APPETIZER

8 ounces / 225 g pork shoulder and belly, cut into 1-inch / 2.5 cm cubes

3 tablespoons / 42 g cold duck fat

1 large egg

1 slice of plain white bread

½ cup / 120 ml heavy cream

¼ teaspoon five-spice powder

1 tablespoon Cognac (optional)

1 teaspoon fresh thyme leaves, finely chopped

½ teaspoon salt

¼ teaspoon white pepper

FOR SERVING

1 baguette

Butter

Cornichons

Mustard, whole grain or Dijon (optional)

Using the grinder attachment on a stand mixer, grind the pork shoulder and belly.

In a large glass bowl, combine the ground pork with the duck fat, then add the egg.

In a small bowl, soak the slice of bread in the cream. Add the softened bread to the pork and mix it until all the bread has broken down and is combined uniformly.

Add the five-spice powder, Cognac, thyme, salt, and pepper and mix until fully incorporated, then place the bowl in the refrigerator for 1 hour.

Preheat the oven to 325°F / 160°C.

Press the meat mixture into a 6 by 4 by 2.5-inch / 15 by 10 by 6.5 cm porcelain terrine with a cover or into a metal 8 by 4-inch / 20 by 10 cm loaf pan. If using a loaf pan, cover the pan with aluminum foil and reduce the temperature of your oven slightly when cooking. Fill a deep sheet pan with several inches of water to create a water bath and then place the pan in the oven. Cook for 1 hour and 30 minutes or until the internal temperature reaches 155°F / 68°C when tested with a digital thermometer. Remove the cover during the last 15 minutes so the top becomes slightly browned.

Remove the pan from the oven and chill overnight in the refrigerator. Slice the cold pâté and serve with a baguette, butter, cornichons, and mustard (if using).

Céleri Rémoulade — Celery Root Salad

I first tried this tangy celery root salad in a café in Sonoma, California, but I did not try making it until we were living in France. It is a common starter salad or side dish to accompany bistro fare. It's also a delicious stand-in for coleslaw and complements fish and chicken dishes. The recipe calls for cornichons, which are tiny little pickles brined in vinegar with herbs. You can grate the celery root, but if you are game to try your knife skills, a julienne gives a crunchier texture to the salad.

SERVES 4

1 large celery root (about 1½ pounds / 680 g) peeled and grated or julienned into fine matchsticks

1 tablespoon white wine vinegar

2 tablespoons Basic Mayonnaise (page 26) or store-bought

2 tablespoons plain yogurt

1 teaspoon Dijon mustard

¼ teaspoon salt

8 cornichons or dill (not sweet) gherkin pickles, sliced into strips

1 tablespoon capers, coarsely diced

1 tablespoon chopped chives

1 tablespoon chopped fresh parsley

A few drops of Tabasco (optional)

In a small bowl, combine the celery root and vinegar. This adds both flavor and helps retain the pale white color of the celery root.

In a large salad or mixing bowl, combine the mayonnaise, yogurt, mustard, and salt, then add the celery root and toss until uniformly mixed. Add the cornichon strips and capers and toss.

Garnish with the chives and parsley. Serve with Tabasco (optional).

Soupe à l'Oignon — French Onion Soup

This soup was conceived in a time when onions were plentiful and inexpensive, and a pot of stock was always simmering on the hearth. It's best if you use a homemade or high-quality store-bought beef broth or stock. A rich chicken broth will also work well but is less authentic to the original. I use a combination of shallots and red and yellow onions for the best texture and color. Sherry vinegar gives the broth a slight tanginess and boosts the flavor of the onions.

SERVES 4

3 tablespoons unsalted butter

2 tablespoons vegetable oil

4 to 6 medium onions, mixed variety, thinly sliced

Salt and freshly ground black pepper

2 tablespoons sherry vinegar or apple cider vinegar

½ cup / 120 ml dry white wine

6 cups / 1.5 L Rich Beef Stock (page 33), Golden Chicken Broth (page 30), or store-bought

2 bay leaves

1 baguette, cut into long slices

Olive oil, for brushing

1 garlic clove, cut in half lengthwise

4 ounces / 115 g Gruyère cheese, grated (about 1 cup)

In a heavy-bottomed stockpot over medium heat, combine the butter and oil and heat until the butter is melted. Reduce the heat and add the onions and salt and pepper. Sauté slowly, until the onions begin to evenly caramelize but not brown. This could take 20 to 25 minutes. When the onions are quite tender and golden, add the vinegar and allow to cook down before adding the wine. Increase the heat to medium and simmer for 5 minutes. Add the broth and bay leaves and simmer on medium low for an additional 20 minutes.

Preheat the oven to broil.

Place the baguette slices on a sheet pan, brush with the oil, and sprinkle with salt and pepper. Toast until golden brown, then rub each baguette slice with the garlic.

Remove the bay leaves before serving. Ladle the soup into ovenproof crocks. Top with the croutons and cheese, then place the crocks on a sheet pan under the broiler until the cheese is melted and bubbly. Serve immediately.

Croque Monsieur

A croque monsieur is traditionally made with ham and cheese between slices of brioche-like bread called *pain de mie*, topped with grated cheese and baked in an oven or fried in a frying pan. My version adds an additional step of cooking the bread first with cream and eggs, much like savory French toast. Serve with a green salad dressed with Classic French Vinaigrette (page 26).

SERVES 2

FOR THE SAUCE

3 cups / 720 ml whole milk

3 tablespoons / 45 g salted butter

3 tablespoons / 23 g all-purpose flour

1 teaspoon Dijon mustard

Salt and freshly ground black pepper

FOR THE SANDWICHES

1 tablespoon butter

1 large egg

¾ cup / 180 ml whole milk

4 slices rustic country bread

2 tablespoons whole-grain mustard

4 slices smoked ham

2 cups / 200 g grated Gruyère cheese

¼ cup / 30 g grated Parmesan cheese

Preheat the oven to 350°F / 180°C. Line a large baking sheet with parchment paper.

Start by making the sauce. In a large microwave-proof measuring cup, heat the milk in the microwave, then set aside.

In a small saucepan over medium heat, melt the butter, then add the flour and cook until bubbly. Once the flour and butter are foamy, slowly add the hot milk and whisk quickly. Add the Dijon mustard and salt and pepper to taste.

To make the sandwiches, in a large sauté pan, melt the butter.

In a shallow bowl, combine the egg and milk and add the bread slices to soak in the same fashion as you would when making French toast. Once the liquid is absorbed, cook the bread slices on both sides in the sauté pan.

Lay the bread slices on the prepared pan. Spread the whole-grain mustard on the inside pieces and lay down two slices of ham on top of each. Add a layer of sauce and then some of the Gruyère cheese. Place the other bread slice on top. On each top slice, add a generous amount of the sauce, more grated Gruyère, and a sprinkling of Parmesan. Place the pan in the oven and cook for 10 to 15 minutes or until the cheese is melted and the top is bubbling.

Boeuf Bourguignon

I recently had the best boeuf bourguignon that I had ever tasted in a *bouillon* restaurant (a restaurant that serves classic French dishes) in Paris. Although I make beef bourguignon frequently, I also order it at restaurants as often as possible to learn more about this rustic and complexly flavored stew of beef and wine. You will find slight variations in recipes, but all are tied together by the use of a full bottle of Burgundy wine that both marinates the beef and creates a beautifully flavorful sauce. While making it might seem complicated with lots of little steps, everything is essentially done in the same pot. Beef bourguignon can be served with steamed potatoes or a creamy root vegetable purée.

SERVES 8

6 pounds / 2.75 kg beef chuck, shank, rump, or shoulder, cut into large chunks

1 large onion, quartered

2 garlic cloves, halved

1 bottle Burgundy wine

2 bay leaves

Salt

Freshly ground black pepper

3 tablespoons all-purpose flour, plus more for seasoning the meat

2 tablespoons butter, plus more as needed

2 tablespoons olive oil, plus more as needed

⅓ cup / 60 g lardons or pancetta

12 whole pearl onions

12 white button mushrooms

3 medium carrots, diced into 1-inch / 2.5 cm cubes

4 medium shallots, finely diced

½ cup / 120 ml Cognac (optional)

1 tablespoon tomato paste

4 cups / 960 ml beef stock

4–6 small peeled whole carrots, steamed

Mashed potato or root vegetable purée for serving

In a large glass bowl, add the beef, onion, garlic, and wine, along with the bay leaves and a pinch of salt. Marinate the beef overnight in the refrigerator or for at least 3 hours.

Remove the beef from the marinade and set on a kitchen towel to dry, reserving the marinade for later. You will want the beef to be completely dry before seasoning with salt and pepper and dusting with flour. Salt and pepper the meat and place the pieces on a shallow platter. Using a fine-mesh strainer, sift the flour evenly over the seasoned meat, turning over the meat to be sure that all sides are evenly coated.

In a large Dutch oven or heavy-bottomed pot over medium heat, warm 1 tablespoon of the butter and oil. Add the lardons and sauté until just beginning to brown. Remove and set on a paper towel. Add more oil as needed and sauté the pearl onions and give a quick sear to the mushrooms. Remove and set aside.

Increase the heat under the pot to medium-high. Add more oil as needed and then brown the beef on all sides. The flour will help create a crust that will keep the meat tender.

Remove the beef and set aside on a tray. Add the diced carrots and shallots to the pot and cook for 2 minutes. Add the Cognac (if using) and deglaze the pan. Then add the tomato paste, followed by the stock.

Return the beef to the pot along with the lardons. Strain the wine marinade over the beef and stock. Bring to a boil, then reduce the heat to low and cook for 3 hours.

Carefully remove the meat and vegetables and reduce the sauce by continuing to cook on high for an additional 10 to 15 minutes. Season with salt and pepper to taste. If you would like a thicker sauce than the reduction provides, you can make a thickening paste. This is done by mashing 1 tablespoon flour with the remaining 1 tablespoon butter on a small plate until combined, a technique called beurre manié. Whisk the butter and flour paste into the sauce and cook until the sauce is thick, about 3 to 5 minutes.

Rewarm the whole carrots in a sauté pan with butter just before plating. When ready to serve, place a spoon of mashed potato purée on each plate followed by the beef and spoon sauce over the top. Arrange the reserved onions and mushrooms around the dish and add the steamed and buttered carrots as a final step.

Oeufs Meurette
Poached Eggs in Red Wine with Crispy Garlic Toasts

This hearty dish of poached eggs in a savory wine sauce originated in Burgundy. History suggests that the dish was created and served in bistros to use up the sauce from leftover beef bourguignon. Served with crispy garlic toast, it can be eaten as an elegant brunch dish or a cozy Sunday evening dinner. The sauce can be made ahead and then heated just before plating.

SERVES 2

1 cup / 240 ml fruity red wine, such as pinot noir or Côte du Rhône

1 ½ cups / 360 ml chicken stock

1 small onion, thinly sliced (about 2 tablespoons)

1 small carrot, quartered

1 celery stalk, chopped into 3-inch / 7.5 cm pieces

1 small garlic clove, thinly sliced

2 or 3 sprigs of thyme, plus 4 for garnish

2 bay leaves

½ teaspoon whole peppercorns

½ cup / 100 g lardons or thick-cut smoked bacon, diced

¼ cup / 60 g salted butter

8 small shallots

¾ cup / 85 g button mushrooms, quartered

2 tablespoons of all-purpose flour

4 large eggs

Olive oil, for drizzling

6 slices of baguette, cut on the diagonal

1 large garlic clove, halved

In a large saucepan over medium-high heat, combine the wine and stock and bring to a boil. Add the onion, carrot, celery, garlic, thyme, bay leaves, and peppercorns. Increase the heat to high and simmer for 15 minutes or until the sauce has reduced by half. Strain the sauce to remove the vegetables and herbs and peppercorns and return the sauce to the pan and set aside.

In a large sauté pan over medium-high heat, cook the lardons until browned, then set aside on a plate. Add 2 tablespoons of the butter to the sauté pan and melt, then add the shallots and sauté until tender. Add the mushrooms, cooking them until they become golden but are still firm.

Put the sauce back on the heat and bring it to a low boil.

Make a paste of the remaining 2 tablespoons butter with the same amount of flour. This is done by mashing the butter with the flour on a small plate until combined, a technique called beurre manié. Then whisk the butter and flour paste into the boiling sauce and cook for 5 minutes, until the sauce is thick and shiny.

Prepare the poached eggs by dropping them one at a time into lightly boiling water (see poaching method on page 59). Remove the eggs with a slotted spoon and rest on a towel.

Preheat the broiler.

Drizzle the oil over the baguette pieces and rub each one with the garlic. Toast under the broiler, turning once, until crispy.

Place 2 of the poached eggs in the center of each plate. Place the lardons and the shallots and mushrooms around the eggs on each plate and pour the hot sauce over them. Garnish with the thyme and serve immediately with the toasted baguettes.

Salade Frisée

Also known as curly endive, frisée is a salad green in the chicory family, known for its bright bitterness and nutty notes. Classically served with a warm vinaigrette, it has somehow made its way from a rustic country salad to a regular on bistro menus. The salad features not only the most delicious, sweet, and tangy dressing but also an expertly poached egg placed in the center and topped with crunchy lardons. *(Pictured on page 61.)*

SERVES 2

⅓ cup / 60 g lardons or thick-cut smoked bacon, chopped into small pieces

Half of a baguette, torn into large pieces

¼ cup / 60 ml olive oil

Sea salt

Freshly ground black pepper

1 large shallot, sliced into thin pieces

¼ cup / 60 ml red wine vinegar

1 tablespoon honey

1 large head of frisée, leaves torn (about 8 cups)

2 large eggs (see note on following page)

2 tablespoons chopped chives (optional)

In a medium sauté pan over medium heat, cook the lardons, tossing occasionally, until browned, 6 to 8 minutes. Set aside on a plate reserving the fat in the pan.

Preheat the oven to 350°F / 180°C.

Place the baguette pieces on a large sheet pan, drizzle with 1 tablespoon of the oil, and sprinkle with salt and pepper. Place the pan in the oven and toast until golden, about 5 minutes.

Return the sauté pan that contains the fat from the lardons back to the stovetop over medium heat and add the shallot, the remaining 3 tablespoons oil, vinegar, and honey. Add the lardons back to the pan. Warm until well combined.

Wash and dry the frisée and set aside.

Prepare the poached eggs by dropping them one at a time into lightly boiling water (see note on the following page). Remove the eggs with a slotted spoon and rest on a towel.

Divide the frisée between two serving bowls and toss with the warm dressing. Add the toasted baguette pieces and top each salad with a warm poached egg.

Finish with black pepper. Garnish with chives.

to poach an egg

Crack one egg into a bowl or onto a saucer.

Bring a pan of water, filled at least 3-inches / 7.5 cm deep, to a simmer.

Gently tip the egg into the pan.

Cook for 2 to 3 minutes, then turn off the heat and leave the egg in the pan for 8 to 10 minutes. The yolk will change color and look firm, but remember, you want the yolk to remain runny.

Lift the egg out of the water with a slotted spoon and drain on a kitchen towel.

tips

The main trick I use when I make poached eggs is to use water that is barely simmering. Fewer bubbles mean less agitation of the water that can break up and disperse the egg whites.

I crack the egg into a cup first, then, when the water is just starting to bubble, I gently slide the egg into the water.

Using a soup spoon, you can spoon water over the yolk so that it cooks evenly. (Remember, you do not want the water to reach a rolling boil, as this can break up the yolk and whites.) Skim the loose or foamy bits from the pan as the egg cooks.

Once you have removed the egg from the water and drained on a towel, trim around the egg with a spoon to achieve a uniform appearance.

Mousse au Chocolat

This creamy and decadent dessert might have entered French culinary history as early as the 17th century, yet it remains iconic as one of the most recognized French desserts. It requires only basic ingredients: good-quality dark chocolate, preferably with a high percentage of cocoa, pure butter, fresh eggs, and sugar.

SERVES 4

6 ounces / 170 g extra-dark chocolate (at least 70% cacao)

5 tablespoons / 70 g salted butter

3 tablespoons / 38 g sugar

4 large eggs

Whipped cream, for topping (optional)

Using a double boiler or a bain-marie over low heat, melt the chocolate and butter and 2 tablespoons of the sugar, stirring gently, until melted and completely smooth. Then remove the pan from the heat and allow the mixture to cool.

Separate the egg whites and egg yolks.

In a large bowl, beat the egg whites and the remaining 1 tablespoon of sugar with a whisk, until stiff peaks form. This can also be done with a stand mixer.

Whisk the yolks lightly with a fork. Temper (see page 18) the slightly warm chocolate mixture into the yolks by blending a small amount of chocolate into the yolks and then gradually adding the rest until well blended.

Folding the whipped egg whites into the melted chocolate should be done in two stages: First, in a large bowl add up to one-third of the whipped egg whites to the chocolate mixture, until the thick chocolate cream becomes lighter, then fold in the rest. A large rubber spatula is by far the best tool for this task, and using large, circular motions will ensure that the bubbles remain intact.

Cool the mousse in the refrigerator for at least 45 minutes or up to 12 hours before serving. Any remaining mousse can be kept in the refrigerator covered with plastic wrap for 2 to 3 days, but it may lose some volume and become denser. Serve in small bowls, ramekins, or teacups.

Tartelettes Tatin aux Pommes — Mini Apple Tarts

Baked with pastry on top and then inverted for serving, this caramelized apple tart dish dates to the 1800s and was the result of a mistake made in a hotel kitchen. My version uses *pâte feuilletée*, or "puff pastry," instead of *pâte brisée*, or "pie pastry." I love the light texture and crunch of the pastry, combined with the tender, slightly tart apples.

**MAKES SIX 4-INCH / 10 CM
SINGLE TARTELETTES**

2 tablespoons / 30 g salted butter, plus more for greasing the pan

¼ cup / 50 g sugar

2 firm green apples, thinly sliced

½ teaspoon ground cinnamon

1 (16-ounce / 450 g) package puff pastry

Vanilla bean ice cream, for serving

Preheat the oven to 350°F / 180°C. Grease six 4-inch / 10 cm tart pans with butter. If using frozen pastry sheets, thaw per instructions.

In a small sauté pan over medium-high heat, melt the butter and sugar and warm until the sugar is dissolved and just begins to caramelize. Add the apples and cook until tender but still holding their shape. Sprinkle with cinnamon. This will only take a minute or two, since the apple slices should be quite thin.

First, cut the puff pastry into six rounds, just slightly larger than your mini-tart pans. You can do this by using a drinking glass as a guide that is slightly larger than the size needed or trace your tart pans leaving about ½ inch / 1.3 cm extra at the rim.

Divide the apple mixture amongst the tart pans, then cover each with a round of puff pastry. Tuck the pastry in, without crimping.

Place the pans in the oven and bake for about 25 minutes, until the pastry is golden.

It's easiest to invert the tartelettes almost right away, so the apples don't get a chance to cool and stick to the tart pans. On a large serving plate, invert each pan, then allow the tarts to cool slightly before serving with ice cream.

Crème Caramel

Crème caramel is a classic French dessert. The custard is silky and not too sweet, and I add Cognac to the sauce to give it a little extra flare. It is usually inverted on a dessert plate, but you can also serve it simply in porcelain mugs or bowls and avoid the fuss of turning out a perfectly formed custard. I'll admit that I am challenged by caramel. I have more stories of burning up sugar than I do of making a great caramel sauce. (And I won't even mention that one time while in the middle of a workshop, I pitched a smoking pan of sugar out the back door unbeknownst to our guests.) However, this recipe is very simple and makes a delicious base for the custard.

SERVES 4

Butter, for greasing the pan

FOR THE SAUCE

1 cup / 200 g sugar

¼ cup / 60 ml water

½ cup / 120 ml heavy cream

Pinch of salt

1 tablespoon Cognac

FOR THE CUSTARD

2 cups / 480 ml whole milk

⅓ cup / 65 g sugar

2 whole eggs, plus 4 egg yolks

1 teaspoon vanilla extract

Preheat the oven to 275°F / 140°C. Grease four porcelain ramekins with butter.

Make the caramel sauce: In a medium sauté pan over medium heat, combine the sugar and water and simmer, swirling the pan but NOT stirring for about 15 minutes, or until a deep amber color is reached. Watch closely so as not to let it burn.

Remove the pan from the heat and slowly add the cream while stirring. Add the salt and Cognac and return to the still-warm burner for another minute while stirring. Transfer to a heat-proof bowl to cool. Store, covered, in the refrigerator and before serving, bring to room temperature or heat in a warm water bath.

To make the custard, in a small saucepan over medium heat, combine the milk and sugar and bring to a low boil, then remove the pan from the heat.

Using a medium bowl and a hand mixer, or a stand mixer fitted with the whisk attachment, whisk the eggs, egg yolks, and vanilla on medium speed. Add a small amount of the warm milk to the eggs to temper the mixture and then, keeping the mixer on low speed, very slowly add the rest of the milk to the eggs, until everything is combined.

Place the ramekins in a shallow baking pan and pour in a few inches of cold water about one-quarter of the way up the exterior of the ramekins. Add a spoonful of the caramel sauce to each. Pour the custard mixture into the ramekins through a small strainer to catch any lumps or eggy bits.

Cover the pan with aluminum foil and bake for 45 minutes. Once done, the custard should be slightly jiggly but firm in the center. Cool before inverting onto individual serving plates.

SUMMER
———
L'ÉTÉ

WE ARRIVED IN FRANCE in the summer of 2010. I remember the view from my in-laws' upper-story windows, seeing slate-grey rooftops, zinc drainpipes, and the many terra-cotta chimney covers. I also remember the loud cries of early-rising seagulls. Normandy was having an unusually warm start to the summer that year, with record temperatures promised before the week was out. I opened the window and leaned out to catch the slight breeze coming from the beach just a few blocks away. I had no idea what time it was, but I do remember posting on my Facebook page the exact picture of what I just described so that friends and family in the United States would know that we had indeed safely arrived.

My husband's parents lived in a bustling upscale resort town on a street that was almost directly across from the daily market that operates every day of the week during the summer, from the early morning hours to just after lunch. Vans and trucks begin to arrive to unload around 7:00 a.m., and it takes only about an hour for the market stalls and tables to be ready and for early shoppers to begin pouring in. It's an event to witness if you ever get the chance. Better yet is the systematic and organized breakdown process at the end of the market day, where, in the blink of an eye, you can't even tell the market had ever been there.

But at the start of the day, the market slowly comes alive. First come the locals, who intentionally arrive ahead of the tourist crowds to get their provisions for the day: fresh produce, cheese, and meats or maybe a pastry to bring back home and enjoy with an espresso before commencing lunch preparations that might span over the next hour or two. It's not unusual to see elderly shoppers with small dogs on leashes, toting market bags that have sustained carrying heavy contents for decades. Greetings are exchanged along with a few moments of local news before carefully wrapped peaches and salads are handed over and coins exchanged. Receipts, if requested, are hastily scribbled numbers on small pieces of white paper. As the morning progresses, lines begin to form at the most popular stands.

The French have varied acknowledgment of and respect for formal queues, and it is not unusual for an impatient shopper to cut in front of people who have been waiting for several minutes. Even if you're biding time in a long line, reaching out and selecting your produce is a big no-no, as is picking up and touching anything you do not fully intend to purchase. You must rely on the eye, nose, and expertise of the vendor, and at most, you can point to the melon or tomato that appeals to you.

Although I will admit that my early memories of our first few weeks in France are a bit foggy, I do remember that a trip to the market across the street quickly became a part of each day. In the first few weeks, my husband returned to the United States to tie up the remaining loose ends and to travel back with our third cat and the last dog. Transporting our pets, the three cats and three dogs, had to be done over two journeys, since the airlines allowed only two animal carriers per trip. So, the two brother cats and the two brother dogs came on the first trip and were already getting into all sorts of trouble with my in-laws. The cats, previously farm cats, did not accept that they should now be confined to a tiny walled garden behind the house and soon learned to scale the brick wall and wander into the courtyard of the primary school on the other side. City living was not for them. Our dogs, Cavalier King Charles Spaniels, chased each other up and down the steep stairs and barked at each new noise—and to them, every noise was apparently new.

The differences of this new culture soon began to surface. The heat wave arrived, and to remain cool, shutters were closed early in the day and not opened again until late evening. The house stayed remarkably comfortable but dark. The combination of newness, jet lag, and the slight worry about an unknown future was emphasized by the confinement to get through the hot days. In the evening, windows were opened and the breeze from the sea would fill the rooms, along with the eager mosquitos. Since there were no window screens, my mother-in-law would put bundles of citronella and geraniums on the windowsills, but nights were still spent swatting the whining nuisances and hiding under thick cotton sheets to minimize the tiny itchy bites that would surely be there in the morning.

It would be months before we could start searching for a house to rent. So, the summer was spent trying to acclimate to our new life as best as we could, until our sea container arrived with our familiar household items, furnishings, personal items, and car.

I can distinctly recall when I felt good and when I felt out of place. I didn't arrive in France striving to become as French as

possible, but I did want to blend in. I had very high hopes that we would be accepted with open arms into a French family I knew only from a couple of vacations and family events like weddings and baptisms. I felt awkward at these formal events, very much lost in the crowd, mainly because of the language barrier. I was also well aware that I was a bit of a strange creature to most people we met: the American wife who didn't speak French, was expecting a child, and who acted and sounded different. I was sure that I was too quiet, flushed too easily, and laughed at the wrong times, as I struggled to appear that I was following conversations during the endlessly long meals and gatherings. I wanted so much for my boys, then five and eleven, not to feel left out or disliked. And being somewhat in culture shock (and very hormonal), I was always on the verge of tears at any given moment. To make things just slightly more complicated, my husband was a modern-day prodigal son, since he had left France when he was twenty-one and now, twenty-seven years later, had arrived back in his hometown with a wife and children in tow.

But at the market, I found unexpected kindness. Because although I was not French, I also made sure not to behave like a tourist. I learned the rules fast and strictly adhered to them. After a morning of exploring and shopping, I felt supercharged. Recipes popped into my head, but, because I didn't yet have a kitchen of my own to experiment in, I could only note and photograph for future inspiration, while we waited to find our own home.

a farm kitchen

The first few months after we moved to Rabbit Hill, our entire focus was doing the work we needed to do to feel settled. It takes time in every new house to figure out how to live in the space, and compared to the small house on the beach road that we rented when we first arrived, our new home, Rabbit Hill, with its high ceilings and expansive tile work throughout, felt like a castle. We decided that the easiest place to start, for so many reasons, was the kitchen. Divided into two rooms in almost a T-shape, there was an awkward concrete step up to the back room, where there was plumbing for a sink and a wall of floor-to-ceiling cabinets. In the front room, there was

plumbing and electrical for a stove. In many French homes, the washer and dryer are also in the kitchen, so there were ample outlets for however we decided to configure things.

The walls were a boring, dingy white, but the dark wood beams added instant appeal and contrast. We decided to paint the walls a bright white color and then began shopping for all the elements: a secondhand professional range, a new European-size (read small) refrigerator, and a 19th-century butcher's table, sturdy enough to hold a small prep sink. Over the next year, we shopped at every *brocante*, or flea market, to find tables and chairs and cabinets

to make a functional space. But what could not be purchased and what had the most dramatic impact in the kitchen was the huge double window and the stunning chiaroscuro light that it beamed onto the counter and throughout the room.

That first summer came and went as we cleaned, painted, and set up, in between chasing around a very active and adventurous two-year-old and entertaining two rapidly growing boys. Starting a farm, despite the setting, was the very last thing on our minds. And a year later, the simple act of adding five hens and a rooster became the first step to our French farm life and the beginning of the next necessary chapter of Rabbit Hill.

Few things in life can teach the same lessons that a farm life can. Succeeding at it, even in small increments, can make you feel like a superhero. There is not one day that is not made better by a visit to the barnyard or pasture, touching a soft nose, getting a loving nudge, hearing a quiet cluck. There cannot be a bad day that ends with a basket of fresh eggs, a bouquet of flowers, or a farm bowl of veggies on the counter.

summer breakfasts

One of the first rituals that emphasizes the start of the summer season is an early morning stroll through the potager garden where I can gather a few vegetables and herbs to make breakfast. In the beginning, it's only a small handful of this and a little bit of that. I love to collect leafy greens, a pinch of the first green beans, and, of course, a freshly laid egg or two. Later in the summer, breakfast is made with decadent heavy sweet tomatoes, thickly sliced on toast. On mornings when my schedule is a bit more rushed, I grab a jar of yogurt and top it with berries and ground flaxseed before running out the door.

POTAGER GREENS WITH EGGS

Gather beet greens, green beans, onion shoots, pea shoots, and eggs. In a small sauté pan, add a dab of butter with a drizzle of olive oil and lightly cook the green beans. I love them cooked only until slightly tender and retaining their fresh crunch. Add the beet greens, onion shoots, and pea shoots before making a space in the center to crack the eggs. Season with salt and pepper and sprinkle with fresh herbs.

THE EPIC TOMATO TOAST

A thick wedge of tomato on toast takes me back to my childhood and to something I enjoyed all through young adulthood and regularly since. It's a simple take on a BLT, which is possibly the first food I ever made when I was five years old. So, no need for the bacon or the lettuce, just a crispy piece of toast, a slice of tomato (at least an inch / 2.5 cm thick!), and a generous full spoon of mayonnaise. For me, another requirement is dried basil, although I can't remember when I first added that. Although I now have summer access to fresh basil, somehow the dried basil in a jar is closer to the nostalgic bites I recall enjoying when I was younger.

Three-Layer Tomato Toast

Tomato toasts have risen to gourmet levels, although I still go back to the three-ingredient version of toast, tomato, and mayonnaise most often (see page 79). But for an occasional treat or special occasion brunch, I recommend the elevated version below. This is a three-layer decadent sandwich of tomato and fresh farm eggs. You will want to attack it with a knife and fork. The bread is toasted in the same pan as the eggs, and then each layer is built.

MAKES 1 SANDWICH

1 tomato

Sea salt

Splash of lemon juice

2 tablespoons salted butter

1 tablespoon olive oil

3 square slices of grainy whole wheat bread

3 large eggs

1 spoonful of mayonnaise (basic is fine, but a red pepper or flavored mayo is lovely, too!)

FOR FINISHING

Assorted fresh herbs, such as chives

Red pepper flakes

Salt and freshly ground black pepper

Slice the tomato into thick slices and add salt to taste, and a squeeze of lemon juice, then set aside.

In a large sauté pan over medium-low heat, melt the butter and oil. Lay the bread slices in the pan and brown on both sides, then set aside.

Fry the eggs either sunny side up or over easy.

Once the eggs are cooked to your preference, layer each toasted slice with a dollop of mayo, a tomato slice, and an egg, then repeat the stack until the top layer is your final egg. Add herbs and spices and salt and pepper to taste.

Lemon-Poppy Seed Crêpes

As a sweet treat or fancy brunch dish, these poppy seed crêpes can be enjoyed in the summer garden with a mimosa on a weekend morning. I use a whole grain flour called *petit épeautre,* which is a semi-whole grain flour, similar to einkorn that has a subtle rustic and nutty flavor. You can also use a 50/50 mix of whole wheat and all-purpose flours. The crêpes are stuffed with a citrusy, creamy filling, made with mascarpone and lemon zest and drizzled with just a touch of honey.

MAKES 6 MEDIUM CRÊPES

FOR THE CRÊPES

2 large eggs

¼ cup / 50 g granulated sugar

2 cups / 480 ml whole milk

2 cups / 250 g einkorn flour

5 tablespoons / 75 g salted butter, melted, plus more for greasing the pan

3 tablespoons / 26 g poppy seeds

FOR THE FILLING

8 ounces / 225 g mascarpone

2 tablespoons lemon juice

1 tablespoon lemon zest

2 tablespoons confectioners' sugar

Blueberries, for topping

Honey, for drizzling

To prepare the batter, in a large bowl, whisk together the eggs, sugar, and milk until combined. Add the flour and whisk rapidly for about 30 seconds, until the batter is smooth. Add the butter and whisk, then add the poppy seeds. Let the batter rest for 30 minutes.

Heat a large frying pan or crêpe pan over medium heat. Using a pastry brush, grease the pan with melted butter and ladle in about ¼ cup of the batter. Tip the pan around to spread the batter evenly; you will want to fill the bottom of the pan to the edges.

Cook the crêpe for 30 seconds to a minute, or until the top has set and has a few bubbles. Flip the crêpe using a spatula and cook for 30 seconds on the remaining side. Continue cooking the remaining crêpes, stacking them on a plate, then set aside to cool.

To prepare the filling, in a food processor, combine the mascarpone, lemon juice and zest, and confectioners' sugar and process until smooth and creamy.

Once the crêpes have cooled, spread the filling on each crêpe and roll or fold. Top with blueberries and drizzle with honey before serving.

la ferme rabbit hill

We are ten years now into our French country farm life, and I don't believe we could ever have visualized any other kind of lifestyle. I think the first thing people who have chosen this path will say is that it is incredibly hard and takes a hefty dose of commitment and perseverance, even at our hobby farm level. We didn't set out to become producers, and we still aren't. We simply thought it would be fun to have a few chickens, then goats, then sheep, then donkeys. Although we share our small bounties of vegetables and flowers and, at times, goat milk, the farm is a folly for us; it entertains us, fulfills us, and as it turns out, feeds our passions and our souls. And as we found out, farm life inevitably makes you into a better human.

Our first chickens came from a cousin who lives in a neighboring village. He had a few little hens and more than enough roosters. In fact, giving us a rooster was the only way he would agree to give us the five little hens. He had roosters to spare and apparently had had his fill of coq au vin. So, among our group of hens was a gorgeous, noble, and quite petite rooster that we named Wellington. Wellington was as charming as he was stunning, with a huge classic tail and vibrant orange and multicolor plumage. He used his loud calling sparingly, crowing in the morning and in the evening when he was calling his girls or, on occasion, when there was the threat of a predator. Between those calls, he would softly cluck, always pointing out the worm or little bug for his ladies before he would take one for himself—he was a true gentleman rooster, through and through.

Goats had always held a fascination for me, from the time I can first remember seeing one at a petting zoo and before I actually understood that goats were a part of agriculture and not an exotic animal. We found our first two girls at a *chèvrerie,* a goat farm, about an hour from our home that produced cheese for a small shop and hosted school groups for tours. To our knowledge, all the goats spent their lives in large groups in a steel shed barn, being bred continuously so they would always be in milk.

It was a lot to take in on our first visit. At this farm, adult goats were normally not adopted out, but we convinced the proprietor to sell us two adult females, so we could have milk and try goat farming. He chose two French alpine girls for us, and we named them Phoebe and Gracie. Phoebe, we were told, was four years old and Gracie was six or seven. We were also told that Phoebe was pregnant, and that we would have milk following the birth of her kid or kids. Gracie, on the other hand, was retired, as she was too old to be bred but would be a good companion for her younger friend. Most of that was not true, except for the part that they would be good friends.

The assurance that Phoebe was pregnant turned out to be false, but it turned out that Gracie was. We joke that Phoebe faked her pregnancy to get off the *chèvrerie.* Perhaps she had gotten word about the potential of a country club life. Gracie, who apparently wasn't too old, gave birth to a strong buckling and the following season we bred Phoebe, who gave birth to surprise twins! And that's where it started. We learned to milk by hand, make yogurt, attempt cheese . . . but the biggest impact for me was the honor and challenge of midwifing the births which turned out to be one of the most amazing things I encountered in farm life.

goat milk yogurt

Once we became a goat farm, finding ways to use the milk became a priority. Beyond making the most delicious goat milk lattes each morning and using the milk in place of cow's milk in just about everything, we still had liters and liters of fresh raw goat's milk each day. We shared the milk with both the kids (goat babies) and our kids (humans) and also made regular deliveries to family members who lived close by. I briefly adventured into cheese making (a story for another time!) and then decided a practical use would be to make goat milk yogurt.

Raw milk is slightly trickier to work with when making yogurt, often producing a thinner consistency due to its variation in natural bacteria, so you have to first pasteurize the milk by bringing it to 145°F / 63°C and holding it at that temperature for 30 minutes. Then, you have to remove it from the heat and stir it, until it has cooled to 40° F / 4°C before you move it to storage in the fridge.

You also need a starter. You can use either a pot of live-culture plain yogurt (full-fat, unsweetened cow's milk yogurt works best) or a packet of starter from a natural foods store. If you use the powdered starter, follow the instructions on the packet. If you are using store-bought live-culture yogurt, you will need ½ cup / 120 g.

Begin by pouring 8 cups / 2 L of pasteurized goat milk into a stainless-steel pot and heat slowly to a gentle boil or about 200°F / 90°C. Remove the pan from the heat and patiently wait for the milk to slowly cool to 115°F / 46°C. Don't be tempted to stir it; just let it rest and cool down. You can also set out your starter yogurt to come to room temperature at the same time. Once the milk comes down in temperature, skim off the milk skin and spoon in the yogurt. Gently blend until there are no large lumps of starter yogurt.

I use a yogurt maker for consistently good results. I pour all the yogurt into individual porcelain pots, set them in the warming bowl, and cover. I set the timer to keep the yogurt at a moderate temperature for 8 to 10 hours, or for whatever time is indicated by the instructions on your own yogurt maker. Check for thickness and consistency only after a minimum of 8 hours and never let it go for longer than 12 hours, or the yogurt might curdle. Once done, store the yogurt containers in the refrigerator for up to 2 weeks. I recommend adding sweetener, such as honey, sugar, agave, or fruit only right before serving.

Farm-Kitchen Muesli

I think everyone loves a little crunchy topping on their morning yogurt. This recipe is a mix of everything I love with just enough sweetness. I find it's a great solution to partial bags of oats and nuts that might be hanging around in the pantry. The aroma while it is toasting in the oven is sweet and lovely. There are absolutely no rules about the quantity of each ingredient, so follow the quantity suggestions given here or create your own version, based on what you have on hand.

MAKES 7½ CUPS / 700 G

¼ cup / 60 ml coconut oil

¼ cup / 60 ml maple syrup (pure syrup without additives) or any sweetener of your choice, such as honey or agave

1 tablespoon ground cinnamon

1 teaspoon vanilla extract (optional)

4 cups / 375 g rolled oats (not instant)

½ cup / 40 g ground flaxseed

1 cup / 60 g pumpkin seeds

1 cup / 60 g sunflower seeds

½ cup / 40 g coarsely chopped almonds

½ cup / 40 g coarsely chopped hazelnuts

OTHER ADDITIONS

Dried fruit, such as raisins, cranberries, or dried apricots. (You will want to toss these in at the end, since dried fruit will get very hard if baked.)

Flaked coconut, seeds, and nuts, such as sesame seeds, chia seeds, pine nuts, walnuts, or any other kinds of nuts

Preheat the oven to 325°F / 160°C. Line a sheet pan with parchment paper.

In a small saucepan over low heat, melt the coconut oil with the maple syrup, then add the cinnamon and vanilla.

In a large glass bowl, combine the oats, flaxseed, pumpkin seeds, sunflower seeds, almonds, and hazelnuts. Add the oil and syrup and mix together. Spread the mixture evenly on the prepared sheet pan and toast for 10 to 15 minutes, stirring once in the middle of the timing.

Store in an airtight container at room temperature for up to 6 months.

the potager

A *potager* is a French kitchen garden. The word translates to "for the soup pot." Potagers can be formal or simple in style, and are designed to provide essential seasonal ingredients, such as herbs, vegetables, and small fruits.

In our first years on the farm, we considered planting a simple field of lavender, but that seemed a bit adventurous, since lavender farms are mostly prevalent in the south of France, and Normandy does not even boast of the smallest level of production.

Partially on a whim, we decided to make our mark as one of the first Basse-Normandie

fermes de lavande (lavender farms), so we planted sixty plants in rocky, wet soil and did our best to establish our plot of folly. Our little field unexpectedly produced more lavender than we could harvest without lots of extra help, but not enough to produce a justifiable amount for lavender products or for essential oils. It did lead to a dreamy occasion, when friends came with clippers and worked in the fields until the summer sun set at almost 11:00 p.m. Bottles of chilled Lillet, a wine-based aperitif, disappeared in an unaccountable way during a sweet candlelit dinner of picnic food that lasted long after the bundles of lavender had been picked and laid out to dry.

It took a few growing seasons to figure out which plants worked and which didn't. Each new summer season, as I learned more, I was able to grow my favorite vegetables (every ingredient needed for ratatouille!), and more recently I started growing flowers for a cutting garden to fill our home with fresh blooms. Each endeavor brought new lessons. In Normandy, tomatoes must be grown under the accelerated warmth of a plastic tarp tunnel or greenhouse; green beans will run rampant in almost any growing situation; and *courgette* (zucchini squash) will grow to gargantuan proportions if you look away and let them go unattended for more than a week.

Still, so many summers later, I find myself testing the rules. I attempt to defy the odds (our local climate and incredibly variant weather). I find myself in the potager at the end of the afternoon, looking after somewhat neglected berry bushes and underpruned plants, hands smelling of the intoxicating aroma of blackcurrants and tomato leaf. I size up the growth and the slowness and wonder whether we will truly have pumpkins by fall or if I will ever see the full ripening of a sweet pepper. The clock is always ticking for a gardener, whose efforts are always fully reliant on the hours of sun, the drops of rain, and the kindness of the wind.

Beyond filling our table and pantry, the summer garden is also about sharing the bounty with baskets filled with eggs, fresh bouquets, tomatoes and peppers, some chard, maybe a massive summer squash. Nothing matches the pleasure of sharing our hard-worked-for produce and blooms that we hand-deliver to friends and family or give to visitors, who never leave the farm empty-handed.

The summer table and the dishes that I make are led by the picks of the day, supplemented by what is abundant at the markets, which are open every day in the summer and not just on the weekends as they are in other seasons. Whatever we don't grow, we know can be easily found there. And knowing that also makes it easier when the goats escape and eat all the berry bushes, or the rabbits finish off all the radishes. Summer on the farm is busy and full, with long days and late sunsets and, if we are lucky, long tables of guests and very cold rosé.

Elderflower Syrup

Before elderberries come elderflowers. These lacy sweetly fragranced flowers appear during the very first weeks of summer. Flowers should be picked when most of the tiny blooms are open, revealing their pale yellow pollen. Give them a good shake before bringing them into your kitchen, since teeny tiny bugs love to inhabit the dainty blooms and stems. I make batches of syrup for desserts and baking and an alcohol version to add to champagne or cocktails. If you wish to add alcohol, a 2:1 ratio of syrup to vodka makes a perfect cordial. The syrup, without the alcohol, can be stored for several months in the fridge if you use citric acid. The addition of vodka will add to the shelf life for up to one year.

MAKES ABOUT 8 CUPS / 2 L

30 elderflower heads

3 unwaxed organic lemons, 1 zested and all sliced into ½-inch / 1.5 cm rounds

2 pounds / 900 g sugar

¼ cup / 50 g citric acid (optional as a preservative)

6 cups / 1.5 L boiling water

In a large bowl, arrange the flower heads and lemon slices in layers.

In a medium pot over medium heat, dissolve the sugar and citric acid (if using) and bring to a low boil. Take the pan off the heat and cool slightly before pouring over the lemon slices and flower heads. Cover the bowl with a kitchen towel and let sit for a minimum of 24 hours and up to 3 days. You can stir occasionally—the perfume-y fragrance is intoxicating! Strain the syrup and transfer it into sterilized bottles or jars.

Elderberry Syrup

If elderflower syrup is a favorite for summer cocktails and fancy desserts, elderberry syrup is her healthy older sister. While elderflowers arrive first during the early weeks of summer, the late summer brings deep purple clusters of tiny juicy berries. The bushes are native to Europe and appear everywhere in hedges, forested areas, and roadsides and for us, all around the perimeter of the farm. In our first summer seasons on the farm, we ignored them and let the birds and occasionally our goats eat all the berries, but once we learned what they were, making syrups and jams became an essential part of our summer. Elderberry syrup is our go-to remedy for colds, sore throats, and immune boosting. It is rich in antioxidants, is a natural antiviral and is believed to have anti-inflammatory benefits. Honey, as a main ingredient, is an exceptional natural antibacterial. If you have foraged berries, you will need to rinse them and remove the berries from the clusters, taking care to remove all the leaves and stem parts. Only the berries are edible, and in very large amounts, the stalks and stems can be toxic. A small bit in your syrup is not of concern but remove as much of the stalks and stems as you can.

MAKES 3 CUPS / 720 ML

1 cup elderberries

3 cups water / 720 ml

1 cinnamon stick

2 cloves

1 teaspoon grated ginger

1 cup / 340 g honey

3 tablespoons / 45 ml bottled lemon juice

In a large pot over low heat, add the berries and water and simmer until the berries are tender enough to mash into a liquid. After about 30 minutes, add the cinnamon stick, cloves, and ginger and simmer for 15 more minutes to infuse. Strain out any bits and the aromatics, then add the honey and lemon juice.

The syrup can be preserved with standard canning methods or processing, but we always tuck the bottle in the back of the fridge, and it lasts us through the cold season. I would advise using it within 6 months if it is kept in the refrigerator.

immune-boosting elderberry tea

This tea is a soothing favorite in our family for sore throats and coughs and general unwellness during cold and flu season. It's a great alcohol-free cough option for young children, who will love the taste. Heat a cup of water and add 1 slice of lemon, 1 tablespoon of honey, and 2 tablespoons of elderberry syrup. Adults can add a spoon or two of brandy!

summer confitures

Fruit jam, also called a confiture, is derived from the French word *confire*, which means to preserve. A confiture requires only three ingredients: fruit, sugar, and acid (lemon juice). In addition, pectin is required but does not have to be an added ingredient, since pectin is present at different levels in fruit (in the skins and seeds) and in lemons.

I love making jam from our berries, plums found at our summer markets, figs late in the season, and our grapes in early fall. For summer jams, ideally you want fruit that is ripe and not past or overripe. Handpicked or market fresh is best as well as being free from any pesticides or treatments, since cooking for a prolonged period can intensify toxins. I like to do batches using 4 to 6 pounds / 1.75 to 2.75 kg of fruit at a time; this yields about eight jam jars.

In most cases, for homemade jam, a simple rule of thumb method is to use as much fruit as you do sugar; that is, a 1:1 ratio. This is a "rule" that consistently makes good jam; however, if you prefer, you can also use less sugar. I am always experimenting to see how much I can reduce the total sugar for the same good result. Classic French confiture recipes will often specify a ratio of 60:40, and there are other elements that come into play. Fruit has its own natural sugar called fructose, or if you want to be more science-y, monosaccharide. Beyond sweetening your confiture, sugar also aids in preservation because of its antibacterial qualities and inevitably helps in thickening the jam as the water content of the fruit is cooked out.

Lemon juice aids in keeping the jam bright and vibrant in flavor. If you need a specific acidity level for preservation, use bottled lemon juice for consistency, since freshly squeezed lemon juice will vary in potency. Lemon juice also prevents sugar from crystallizing, and as I previously mentioned, it contains pectin in its peels and seeds. You can even make a natural thickener sachet by putting a bundle of lemon seeds and peels in a small square of cotton cheesecloth, tying with a string, and using it like a tea bag in your jam pan. I find this method is preferable to using packaged pectin powder, or jam sugar, that contains additional ingredients and most likely uses refined sugar.

Each adventure into making confiture creates a different end result, and even after carefully following instructions, you can end up with a stunning batch of jam or a failed one, just due to the natural variances in the ingredients. I have made many "sauces" that were intended to be jam when it just didn't gel completely. I have also made a few really thick, gummy ones, too. I have heard that you can reheat overly firm jam with a drizzle of hot water, but I am not certain what this would do as far as re-preserving or canning it again. If you find yourself with very thick jam, it makes a delicious topping with Brie or Camembert on a cracker on a cheese board and can also be used by the spoonful to enhance a savory sauce. I love adding berry jams to sauces for duck or meats with a splash of sherry vinegar to balance the sweetness.

I will always believe that the best part of jam making is the smell of the stewing fruit and the anticipation of something preserved to be used for later or for sharing a jar with a friend or neighbor. Putting away a little taste of summer that can be enjoyed year-round.

Confiture aux Trois Baies — Three-Berry Jam

Around the farm, we not only grow berries but also have wild berries that were planted decades ago in the hedges. In our potager, we have *cassis*, or blackcurrants, and *groseille*, or red currants; in the hedges, we have elderberries and blackberries. A combination of these berries in this jam is a fragrant and deeply flavored, slightly tart medley of perfection. You can make lightly sweet, savory sauces for duck or white meats or a classic confiture like the recipe below. Either way, this jam is versatile and delicious.

MAKES 6 PINT JARS / 6 HALF LITER JARS

36 ounces / 1 kg mixed berries, such as elderberries, blackberries, and currants

4 cups / 800 g organic unrefined sugar

3 tablespoons / 45 ml lemon juice

Begin by preparing the fruit, which should be washed and sorted to remove stems or small bits of leaves.

In a copper confiture pan or a large but shallow pot, add the berries and take a moment to crush them with a spoon or masher. A whisk also works well for this. Begin warming the smashed berries over low heat, then add the sugar. Simmer to an eventual boil for a total simmer time of 30 minutes, stirring occasionally to combine until the sugar is completely dissolved. Adjust the heat as needed. It is okay for the jam to bubble as it simmers, but it's best not to allow it to go to a full rolling boil.

After 30 minutes, turn off the heat and allow the jam to sit for 30 minutes. It will still be syrupy and not set. Turn the heat to low to reheat the jam. Add the lemon juice, and heat for an additional 30 minutes. The staggered cooking time gives the natural pectin in the seeds the time needed to be released and aids in setting the jam as it cools.

If you are planning on canning, this is the perfect time to prepare jars, lids, and seals and to gather a funnel, ladle, and jar labels. I set these on a clean towel on the counter so that everything is ready and within arm's reach.

As a final step, bring the jam to a full boil before putting it into prepared jars for canning or for storing in the refrigerator or freezer. Refer to your canning guide for safe storage at room temperature. Once opened, jam can be kept in the refrigerator for up to 6 months or in the freezer for up to 1 year.

Rhubarbe Confite

Since the first time making this deliciously vibrant rhubarb in syrup or "confite," I have been smitten with this method. What I love about it is that it honors a generations-old practice of slow cooking, using the residual heat from the stove in times when one had to utilize what was available. Because of the very slow and timed process, the finished confite is a deep jewel color and is wonderfully textured. It can be used simply on toast or more decadently in a dessert or pastry.

MAKES 2 QUARTS / 2 L

4½ pounds / 2 kg rhubarb

4½ pounds / 2 kg organic sugar

notes

If you wish to make a smaller or greater quantity, use equal parts of the rhubarb and sugar.

If you overcook, it will still be delicious but will be cloudier and paler in color. The goal is that the rhubarb still has texture and is candied rather than mushy.

Wash and prepare the rhubarb by removing the leaves and ends and chopping the stalks into uniform 2-inch / 5 cm pieces. Layer the rhubarb and sugar in a copper confiture pan or large shallow pot. Cover with a lid and set on the back of the stove for 24 hours. During this time, the rhubarb will release juices.

This next part may seem laborious, but it really isn't. Place the pan over low heat. Warm the rhubarb and sugar slowly, not allowing it to bubble or boil, for 20 to 30 minutes. It's best not to cover it while it's warming, since you might lose track and it could heat up too much. Also, there is no need to stir it. Just allow it to warm gently. Once the warming time has passed, turn off the heat, cover, and set aside. That's all for the first day.

The next morning, put the pan back on the stovetop and heat on low for 10 to 15 minutes. (Be sure to set a timer so that you don't forget!) Then turn off the heat, cover, and let it sit. A few hours later, turn it on again and cook it in the same way. Repeat every few hours, about 4 to 6 times total, then let it rest again overnight.

On day three, you will heat the rhubarb and sugar slightly longer and allow it to bubble before turning it off. This part of the recipe is done completely by sight, but usually takes 2 to 3 rounds of heating to a simmer. Once the rhubarb confite is bright in color and the syrup is thick, it is done.

If you are planning on canning, follow the directions and methods for standard jam making. You will need approximately four 1-pint / 475 ml jars. Prepare the jars, lids, and seals and gather a funnel, ladle, and labels. I set these on a clean towel on the counter so that everything is ready and within arm's reach.

Preserves can be kept in the refrigerator for up to 6 months or in the freezer for up to 1 year.

Summer Potager Tomato Sauce

After patiently waiting for our tomatoes to appear and ripen, a celebration of the harvest is a requirement! By late summer, every surface in the kitchen is filled with beautifully ripe tomatoes. To enhance the vibrant tomato sweetness and acidity, I love adding in loads of rustic and salty elements. This sauce is a perfect marinara base sauce from which many other variations can be made. *(Pictured on page 108.)*

MAKES ABOUT 6 CUPS / 1.5 L

About 6 pounds / 2.75 kg tomatoes, any variety or a mix

¼ cup / 60 ml extra-virgin olive oil

4 garlic cloves, cut into very thin slivers

1 medium red onion, finely diced

1 tablespoon lemon juice

Pinch of sugar

2 tablespoons herbes de Provence

Salt and freshly ground black pepper

To easily remove the tomato skins, cut an × in the bottom of each tomato. Fill a large pot with water and bring to a boil over high heat. Drop the tomatoes into the water and boil for 3 minutes. Remove the tomatoes from the pot and once they have cooled, remove the skins. If you are making a smooth sauce, you can leave the skins on, since you will use an immersion blender as a last step.

In a large heavy-bottomed sauce pot over medium heat, add the oil, garlic, and onion. Cook until tender and then add the tomatoes, breaking them apart with a wooden spoon. Add the lemon juice and sugar and continue to cook down and thicken. The sauce can simmer for several hours to achieve the desired consistency. Once thick, add the herbes de Provence and continue to cook for one more hour, adding salt and pepper to taste.

If you are planning on canning, this is the perfect time to prepare jars, lids, and seals and to gather a funnel, ladle, and jar labels. I set these on a clean towel on the counter so that everything is ready and within arm's reach. I like to use pint / 475 ml size jars for specialty sauces and quart / L size for all-purpose sauces.

MY FAVORITE VARIATIONS

Puttanesca Sauce

TO THE BASE SAUCE, ADD:

¼ cup / 40 g each chopped kalamata olives and French green olives

1 tablespoon capers, drained

4 to 6 anchovy fillets, crushed to a paste

Salt and freshly ground black pepper, to taste

Red pepper flakes, to taste

Arrabbiata Sauce

TO THE BASE SAUCE, ADD:

1 cup / 150 g mixed finely chopped, hot and sweet peppers, sautéed in 1 tablespoon olive oil

1 tablespoon hot chili flakes

Add the ingredients when the base sauce has almost reached the thickness and texture desired and simmer for another 25 minutes before jarring the finished sauce.

Roasted Vegetable Sauce

TO THE BASE SAUCE, ADD:

1 small eggplant

1 medium red pepper

1 small zucchini

1 medium onion

5 garlic cloves

Olive oil, for drizzling

1 or 2 sprigs each of fresh rosemary and thyme, stems removed.

Coarsely chop the vegetables in equal sizes and place them on a large sheet pan. Drizzle with oil, and roast in a 425°F / 220°C oven for 25 minutes or until evenly roasted, depending on the size of the veggies. Scrape the pan into the base sauce and use an immersion blender to combine until smooth. Alternately, you can make a chunkier sauce by skipping this step.

Tagine Sauce

TO THE BASE SAUCE, ADD:

2 tablespoons store-bought spices for Kefta (also called Kafta) or make your own by mixing together 1 tablespoon each of ground cinnamon and smoked paprika, and 1 teaspoon each of ground coriander, ground cumin, garlic powder, and ground marjoram

In a small saucepan, dry toast the spices just until they begin to warm. Add the spices to the base sauce. This sauce is a delicious and time-saving, make-ahead sauce for tagine dishes, chicken, and vegetables.

Roasted Tomato Ketchup

When faced with an abundance of tomatoes, and at the same time, with a pantry full of tomato sauce and maybe even a freezer filled with frozen tomatoes, only one thing comes to mind—ketchup. Ketchup is a staple in every American home and is still considered somewhat of a novelty condiment in France. You can always find a basic ketchup at a local grocery store but rarely a gourmet type, and I think that once you make your own at home, there will be no turning back!

MAKES ABOUT 6 CUPS / 1.5 L, DEPENDING ON HOW MUCH YOU COOK IT DOWN

Olive oil, for drizzling

About 6 pounds / 2.75 kg thick-fleshed tomatoes, such as beefsteaks or Romas

½ cup / 100 g dark brown sugar

½ cup / 120 ml apple cider vinegar

1 teaspoon celery salt

½ teaspoon Worcestershire sauce

1 teaspoon granulated garlic

5 cloves

2 tablespoons smoked paprika

1 tablespoon smoked hot chili powder (optional)

Preheat the oven to 425°F / 220°C. Prepare a sheet pan by drizzling it with the oil.

Slice the smaller tomatoes in half and quarter the larger ones.

Place the tomatoes on the prepared pan and roast for 25 minutes.

Remove the pan from the oven and tip the tomatoes into a large saucepan over medium heat. Cook for 15 minutes before blending with an immersion blender in the pan or a food processor. In the same pan, then add the brown sugar, vinegar, celery salt, Worcestershire sauce, garlic, cloves, smoked paprika, and chili powder (if using). Simmer for 1 to 3 hours or until the ketchup reaches the desired thickness. The exact time will vary based on the water or juice level of the tomatoes. The average time is around 3 hours.

You can preserve the ketchup for later use by using a traditional canning method but be aware of the acidity level in the tomatoes; if it is on the low side, you will want to add lemon juice to boost it or add citric acid for long-term preservation. Once opened, the ketchup should be used within a few weeks, since it lacks the preservatives that are found in processed ketchup. For this reason, I recommend jarring it in small batches or condiment-size jars that will be used quickly rather than a very large amount in a bigger jar.

Pickled Peppers

There are several pantry staples that are less frequently found on the grocery store shelves in Normandy. Hot and spicy peppers are one of them. As I love a flavorful and potently hot pepper at times, my craving led to the necessity of making them! My first batches were made from Moroccan hot peppers that I discovered at our market. Soon after, I sourced seeds to grow several types of hot peppers in our potager. I have been known to sneak a few dried peppers from travels into my bags for the precious seeds within, and I love growing a few varieties each summer that yield different levels of heat and flavor.

This simple method is for a single batch; most often I double it. You can also add other fresh vegetables, such as carrots, bell peppers, cauliflower, and onions. I use pickled peppers on egg dishes, in sandwiches and burgers, and in summer salads for the perfect kick of heat!

MAKES ABOUT 1 QUART / 960 ML

4 cups / around 700 g mix of peppers of your choice, chopped into pieces or rings

2 garlic cloves

2 cups / 480 ml white vinegar

1 cup / 240 ml water

1 teaspoon salt

1 tablespoon sugar

Prepare your jars (one 1-quart / 1 L jar or two 1-pint / 500 ml jars) by washing them in hot water and then setting them aside. For this recipe, there is no need to sterilize them; just run them through the dishwasher or hand wash.

For hotter peppers, remove the seeds and interior parts of the pepper (called glands). Fill each jar with the pepper rings, pressing down and squeezing in as many as you can. Place 2 garlic cloves in the quart jar, or 1 in each of the pint jars.

In a nonreactive saucepan over medium-high heat, add the vinegar, water, salt, and sugar, and bring to a low boil. Reduce the heat to low and simmer for about 10 minutes, then remove the pan from the heat.

Pour the vinegar mixture into each jar, leaving about ½ inch / 1.3 cm of headspace before tightly sealing. You can put the jar in the refrigerator once cooled and the peppers will last almost indefinitely. You can also process the jars in a canner for 15 minutes for larger jars and 10 minutes for smaller jars. Once opened, store in the refrigerator. Be sure that the contents remain covered or submerged in the pickling liquid.

Cucumber-Yogurt Soup

This soup reminds me of my love for Indian raita, which is a yogurt-based condiment served with rice dishes and flatbreads. I love the simplicity of this dish, which makes it an easy hot weather dinner that doesn't take a lot of time or effort with the bonus of using summer vegetables fresh from the farm garden. Don't be fooled by its light flavors and subtle aromatics; this soup is hearty and deliciously filling!

SERVES 4

1 large English or seedless cucumber, finely chopped

Sea salt

1½ cups / 300 g cherry tomatoes (a mix of colors), quartered or halved

2 cups / 500 g full-fat Greek yogurt

Freshly ground black pepper

1 tablespoon ground cumin

1 tablespoon fresh basil, finely chopped, plus more for garnish

2 tablespoons fresh mint, finely chopped, plus more for garnish

1 tablespoon Nigella seeds, for garnish

Naan or pita bread, for serving

Sprinkle the finely chopped cucumber with sea salt and set aside.

Put the quartered or halved cherry tomatoes into a large bowl. Drain the excess moisture from the cucumbers and add to the chopped tomatoes, reserving a small amount to place on top of the soup. Cover with the yogurt and add a pinch more sea salt and black pepper to taste.

In a small pan over low heat, add the cumin and heat just until it begins to toast. Warming aromatic spices enhances their flavor that is sometimes lost when in powder form. You will smell the aroma of the cumin once it is ready. Add the warm cumin to the yogurt mixture. Add the basil and mint to the soup and whisk with a fork. Finish the soup with the reserved chopped cucumber and tomatoes.

Serve cold, garnished with basil, mint, and a sprinkling of Nigella seeds, alongside flat breads like naan or pita.

The soup can be stored in an airtight container in the refrigerator but should be served within 1 to 2 days for the best flavor and texture.

Ceviche with Shrimp and Melon

Fresh, clean flavors and perfect acidity make ceviche one of the best options for a light dinner or palette-opening summer appetizer. Ancient versions were made by adding fermented juices to raw fish, while contemporary versions use the acid from fresh citrus juice to "cure" the fish and thus make it safe for consumption. Various fresh herbs and spices are used along with cold vegetables and fruit. Always select fresh fish and use it on the same day it's purchased.

**SERVES 4 TO 6,
AS AN APPETIZER**

1 pound / 450 g fresh cod, sea bass, or mahi-mahi, cut into ¼-inch / 6 mm cubes, cleaned and boned

½ pound / 225 g cooked tiny shrimp (61/70 count or diced larger shrimp)

1 green chili pepper, finely chopped

½ medium red onion, chopped into small, very thin slices

¾ cup / 180 ml fresh lime juice

½ cup / 70 g cantaloupe, or honeydew melon, finely diced

½ cup / 70 g English or seedless cucumber, finely diced

¼ cup / 30 g fennel, diced, with fronds reserved for garnish

Salt and freshly ground black pepper

¼ cup / 10 g chopped fresh cilantro, for garnish

In a large glass bowl, combine the fish, shrimp, chili pepper, and onion. Add the lime juice and allow to marinate in the refrigerator for 15 to 30 minutes. It can go longer, but the texture of the fish will become firmer and more opaque.

Add the melon, cucumber, and fennel. Add salt and pepper to taste.

Serve very cold, garnished with fennel fronds and cilantro.

The ceviche can be stored in an airtight container in the refrigerator for up to 2 days, but it is best when served fresh.

Creamy Cold Tomato Soup with Pickled Vegetables

Sometimes the best recipes are the results of "happy accidents": a combination of newly matched ingredients or the creative use of leftovers. The French have a classic tomato salad that is simply dressed with shallots and wine vinegar or apple cider vinegar, and after a meal, there could be a platter of perfectly seasoned and flavorful tomato slices left over. Once cut, tomatoes suffer if put in the refrigerator (or, in my opinion, if ever put in the refrigerator), so what can be done with a few portions of *salade aux tomates*? *Et voila!* This is the easiest quick and flavorful cold tomato soup that makes a perfect starter or amuse-bouche. The addition of pickled vegetables elevates it to a pretty presentation of vibrant summer flavors!

SERVES 6 AS AN APPETIZER

FOR THE PICKLED VEGETABLES

1 cup Farm Stand Summer Vegetable Corn Salad (page 139)

1 tablespoon apple cider vinegar

FOR THE SOUP

4 to 5 large thick-fleshed tomatoes, such as beefsteaks or Romas, sliced into large wedges

2 shallots, finely diced

2 tablespoons chopped fresh parsley, plus more for garnish

3 tablespoons / 45 ml apple cider vinegar

1 tablespoon olive oil

¼ cup / 60 g crème fraîche or full-fat sour cream

½ teaspoon salt

Chopped chives, for garnish

To make the pickled vegetables, in a small bowl, combine the corn salad and vinegar. Set aside to marinate for 30 minutes.

To make the soup, in a large glass bowl, combine the tomatoes, salt, shallots, and parsley.

In a small bowl, whisk together the vinegar and oil and pour over the tomatoes. Cover the bowl and let sit at room temperature for about an hour. After the time has passed, in a blender on high speed, blend the tomato mixture for about 1 minute, until it is perfectly smooth. Add the crème fraîche and blend for 30 more seconds before pouring into shallow bowls.

Since this dish is served as an appetizer, you are only making small servings. Spoon one heaping soup spoonful of pickled vegetables in the center of each soup serving, then garnish with the parsley and chives.

Les Moules d'Été au Pastis

Steamed Mussels with Pernod Cream Sauce

Every summer we eagerly await the arrival of local Normandy mussels. Although we enjoy a long season with mussels harvested from varying locations, there is a small window, where they are harvested not far from us in the area of the D-Day beaches. One beach, in particular, called Utah Beach boasts some of the best mussels we have ever tasted. The summer we discovered them, we ate mussels five times over a period of two weeks, during the time when they were available. The problem is, they are also recognized for their superiority by chefs and foodies, so the competition is rough. You have to be very good friends with your fishmonger to get the secret text message, "*Les moules sont arrivées!*" I can't take credit for this dish, as I have rarely made it. I have, however, been the sous chef for it many times. It's a recipe from my father-in-law's repertoire and hence is always cooked by his son, while I stand close by, holding a glass of wine—exactly as he would have wanted it.

SERVES 4

6¾ pounds / 3 kg mussels

2½ tablespoons butter

1 tablespoon olive oil

3 medium shallots, finely diced

1 teaspoon herbes de Provence

Several sprigs of fresh thyme

2 tablespoons Pernod or any anise-flavored liqueur

½ bottle dry white wine

2 cups / 480 ml heavy cream

Baguette and butter, for serving

Rinse and clean the mussels, removing small bits of seaweed or debris from the shells. Fresh mussels should be tightly closed and smell of the sea, so be sure to discard any that are open or cracked.

In a very large pot over medium heat, melt the butter with the oil, add the shallots, and cook until tender. Add the herbes de Provence and thyme, then add the Pernod and deglaze the pan. Increase the heat to high and add the white wine. Bring the liquid to a full rolling boil, then add the mussels and cover. Wait for 3 minutes and then shake the pot from side to side. Remove the cover and turn the mussels around in the pot with a slotted spoon, pulling the open ones to the top. Cover again and cook for 3 more minutes.

Mussels usually take 5 to 8 minutes in total to cook. Small ones will cook very quickly and if overcooked will have a mealy texture. Once the majority are opened, you can remove the cooked mussels with a slotted spoon and place them in a large serving bowl. Be sure to discard any mussels that do not open.

Add the cream to the cooking broth and reduce for about 5 minutes or until the sauce is creamy and sticks to the back of a spoon. Ladle the hot creamy sauce over the mussels and then pour the rest into a small pitcher to serve table side or to reheat for second courses. Always serve with plenty of fresh baguette to soak up the delicious sauce and plenty of napkins!

Grilled Mackerel with Ratatouille

Ratatouille is a summer staple as a flavorful side or main dish that uses bountiful vegetables from the garden and can be made ahead. It couples well with poultry and is stunning with spicy merguez sausage. If it is a hot evening and you already have a batch prepared and ready to warm up (or sometimes even served cold!), the addition of a piece of grilled fish makes the perfect meal. Mackerel is an ideal fish for summer grilling, since it cooks quickly and needs only a small amount of salt and pepper and a drizzle of olive oil before cooking. I love adding a spoon of zesty gremolata that features fresh herbs and lemon to the grilled fish. Other additions I love to add before baking are capers, green olives, and anchovies. I believe that there are no hard-set rules for the amount of each vegetable that you use, so feel free to utilize whatever you have in the garden.

SERVES 4 TO 6

FOR THE RATATOUILLE

2 tablespoons olive oil, plus more for drizzling

1 large red onion, diced

2 eggplants, cubed

3 bell peppers, any color, diced

2 large zucchini, cubed

2 yellow squash, cubed

4 garlic cloves, thinly sliced

2 cups / 400 g fresh tomatoes, diced

1 tablespoon herbes de Provence

Salt and freshly ground black pepper

1 (6-ounce / 170 g) piece mackerel per person

FOR THE GREMOLATA

1 tablespoon dill or fennel fronds

2 tablespoons capers

1 teaspoon lemon zest

½ teaspoon lemon juice

1 tablespoon chopped fresh parsley

½ tablespoon olive oil

Preheat the oven to 325°F / 160°C.

To make the ratatouille, in a large Dutch oven or heavy-bottomed ovenproof pot over medium heat, warm the oil. Add the onion and sauté until translucent.

To the same pot, add the eggplant and peppers and cook on medium heat until lightly seared. Once they begin to brown slightly, add the zucchini, squash, and garlic. Cook over low heat for 20 to 25 minutes before adding the tomatoes and herbes de Provence. Combine by folding the ingredients several times. Drizzle a little oil over the top and season with salt and pepper.

Cover the pot and cook the ratatouille in the oven for 45 minutes. The time in the oven allows the stewing of the vegetables, which results in a thicker and richer final dish.

To prepare the mackerel, pat each fillet with a paper towel to dry before drizzling with a small amount of oil. Place the fish skin-side-down on a hot plancha or grill. Two minutes on each side is sufficient, as the flesh is usually quite thin. Alternatively, you can fry the fish in a pan on your stovetop.

To make the gremolata, in a small bowl, chop and combine the fronds, capers, lemon zest, and juice. Mix with the parsley and finish with the oil.

Serve each piece of mackerel with a spoon of gremolata accompanied by the ratatouille on each individual plate or on a single serving platter.

Savory Paris-Brest with Vegetables and Prawns

Paris-Brest is a dessert made by creating a round ring of choux pastry that is filled with a sweet cream filling normally flavored with praline. The name comes from the original pastry that was created to commemorate a bike race from Paris to Brest back in 1910. My version is a savory spin-off, excuse the pun, that features fresh ingredients from the summer potager garden and is filled with a creamy herb-cheese filling. Equal parts whimsical and upscale, this dish is wonderful as a starter or in a larger format for a special summer celebration meal or garden party. *(Pictured on page 127.)*

MAKES 4 LARGE OR 6 SMALL CHOUX RINGS

FOR THE PASTRY

1 cup / 240 ml water or milk, or ½ cup / 120 ml of both

6 tablespoons / 90 g unsalted butter, cut into ½-inch / 1.5 cm cubes

½ teaspoon salt

1 cup plus 1 tablespoon / 128 g all-purpose flour

4 large eggs

Prepare a mise en place of the cooked prawns, fresh and blanched vegetables, and herbs, and keep these ingredients chilled until ready to assemble.

In a medium saucepan over high heat, combine the water, butter, and salt. Cook until the liquid comes to a rolling boil and the butter has fully melted, about 2 minutes.

Remove the pan from the heat and add the flour. Mix in the flour with a spoon or spatula until no lumps remain. Return the pan to medium-high heat and cook, stirring very frequently, until the dough begins to come together.

Once you remove the pan from the heat, you can complete the choux pastry by using either a stand mixer, fitted with the dough hook or batter attachment, or by hand. To use a stand mixer: transfer the dough to the bowl and whisk for 3 to 5 minutes, allowing the dough to cool slightly in preparation for adding the eggs.

Add the eggs one at a time, making sure each is fully beaten into the dough before adding the next; it can help to start the mixer at medium-low speed for the first egg and then increase the speed to medium once the choux batter begins to come together. Scrape down the sides of the bowl, then mix once more at medium speed just to ensure the choux batter is fully mixed, about 5 seconds.

To mix by hand, leave the dough to cool in the pan, stirring frequently. Add the eggs one at a time, stirring well and vigorously between additions, until each egg is fully incorporated before adding the next. Continue until a smooth, shiny paste forms. This will take rapid mixing and a little perseverance.

FOR ASSEMBLY

4 to 6 extra-large prawns, cooked and chilled

4 to 6 whole radishes, with partial stems on

4 to 6 small carrots, with partial stems on, blanched and chilled

12 to 18 snow peas

1 cup / 240 g herbed goat cheese spread, such as Boursin or Tartare

FOR THE GARNISH

Capers

Diced spring onions

Chopped fresh parsley or any fresh summer herbs

Dill and fennel fronds

Cracked pink peppercorns

Use the choux pastry right away or keep at room temperature for up to 2 hours. If not using right away, fill a pastry or resealable plastic bag and set aside.

Line a baking sheet with parchment paper. Depending on the size of the choux pastry ring you want to make, you can trace circles on a piece of parchment baking paper and then pipe the choux pastry using a large tip or in a 1-inch / 2.5 cm circle onto the parchment. Remember that the pastry will more than double in size, so a 4½-inch / 11.5 cm ring will expand to be the size of a standard bagel. If you are making an appetizer size, pipe a ring with a maximum diameter of 3 inches / 7.5 cm.

Preheat the oven to 400°F / 200°C.

Place the pan in the oven and bake for 10 minutes. Reduce the oven temperature to 350°F / 180°C and continue baking for 15 minutes. The exterior of the rings should be golden brown, and the interior should be tender and pale yellow. Remove the pan from the oven and set aside to cool on a wire rack.

To assemble the rings, slice the rings in a bagel-like fashion. After slicing the rings, pipe a generous amount of Boursin onto the bottom piece of each pastry, then replace the top piece. Fill the center of each ring just enough to hold the vegetables and prawns. Add 1 prawn per serving and fill the center of each ring with the cold vegetables. Garnish with the capers, spring onions, parsley, fronds, and peppercorns.

Tian of Summer Vegetables

This dish is a beautiful celebration of the garden in an elegant presentation that is deceivingly simple to create. Referred to as a tian, it features neatly layered baked vegetables. If you have a mandoline, it is an essential tool to cut the vegetables to uniform thickness, but this can also be achieved with the use of a very sharp chef's knife. The amounts of each ingredient are flexible, but the more variety in color the better. Be prepared to experiment with arranging the slices of vegetables; this can be done in a round or rectangular roasting pan. The goal is to cut the vegetables in equal-diameter slices so they cook evenly and make a lovely spiral or layered shape.

SERVES 4 TO 6

2 cups / 480 ml Arrabbiata Sauce (page 107)

2 small zucchini

1 yellow squash

2 medium eggplants

3 large jarred roasted peppers, quartered or cut into wide slices if whole

¼ cup / 60 ml olive oil

2 tablespoons pesto

2 tablespoons jarred sun-dried tomatoes in oil, drained

Grilled meat or sausage, for serving (optional)

Cut the vegetables into uniform sizes. You will want to pack them in tightly in the pattern that you choose, since they will shrink slightly while cooking. Once you have all the vegetables cut into equal thickness and diameter, I find it helps to "dry fit" them into the pan just to see if you need to add more or less of any one type.

Using an 8- to 10-inch / 20 to 25 cm round baking pan or deep pie dish, begin by adding the arrabbiata sauce to the bottom of the pan. Then add the zucchini, squash, and eggplant in a layered or circular pattern. Once you have a uniform pattern, push the roasted pepper slices in between the vegetable slices to fill the gaps.

Preheat the oven to 325°F / 160°C.

Mix the oil with the pesto and drizzle over the vegetables. Fill the gaps between the layers with drained sun-dried tomatoes.

Place the pan in the oven and roast for 1 hour, then check the tenderness of the vegetables and overall browning. You can add more time, checking in 10-minute increments. If you think the dish is becoming too browned, you can finish the final cook time by covering the pan with aluminum foil. Serve warm with grilled meat or sausage if you wish.

Miso Eggplant with Wheat Berries

A few summers ago, we had more eggplants than I could keep up with. Not only were they plentiful but they also all became ripe at the very same time. Luckily, there are countless ways to utilize them since this vegetable adapts to so many different types of flavors. I love serving eggplant with the contrasting texture of the plump and firm wheat berries, which have a hearty and nutty flavor that pairs with the salty sweet tones of miso in this recipe.

SERVES 2

2 tablespoons olive oil

2 medium eggplants, cut into 1-inch / 2.5 cm cubes

2 tablespoons white miso paste

1 tablespoon sesame oil

½ tablespoon fresh ginger, minced

1 tablespoon tamari or regular soy sauce

1 tablespoon rice vinegar

1 tablespoon honey

2 tablespoons hot water

2 cups / 500 g cooked wheat berries or farro

1 tablespoon chopped red onion

1 tablespoon rice vinegar

2 tablespoons olive oil

Toasted pine nuts

Toasted sesame seeds

Chopped fresh cilantro

In a medium sauté pan over medium-high heat, warm the olive oil and once the pan is almost smoking hot, add the eggplant. Once seared, take the pan off the heat and prepare the sauce.

In a small glass bowl, whisk together the miso paste, sesame oil, ginger, soy sauce, vinegar, and honey, then drizzle the hot water over the mixture. Set aside.

Place the pan back on medium heat and add the sauce. Toss quickly, heat for about 30 seconds, then set the pan aside.

In a shallow bowl toss the cooked wheat berries with the red onion, vinegar, and olive oil. Top with the eggplant and then garnish with toasted pine nuts, sesame seeds, and cilantro.

cooking wheat berries

I love this simple, high-fiber grain in summer salads and even as an ingredient in breakfast dishes. You can cook large batches at a time and store them in the refrigerator for easy use.

If you have difficulty finding wheat berries, you can substitute farro, which is similar in taste and only slightly different in texture. Both grains come in two types: pearled or whole. Pearled means that the outer layer or bran has been removed; this does not reduce the nutritional value and on the plus side, reduces the overall cooking time.

Before using, rinse the wheat berries in a fine-mesh colander. Fill a large pot with salted water over high heat and bring to a boil. Add 2 to 3 cups / 400 to 600 g of wheat berries or farro and cook until tender. Wheat berries will be chewy in texture but should not be hard, and farro should be cooked until al dente and not split open and mushy.

Whole wheat berries and farro will take 40 to 45 minutes to cook, while pearled versions will take 10 to 15 minutes. Keep the grains cooking at a low boil (much like rice) and covered. Test every 5 to 10 minutes after the average cooking time has passed. Drain the remaining water and allow to cool to room temperature.

Salade Potagère de Haricots Verts

Summer Vegetable Salad

This cold vegetable salad is a culmination of everything I love in the summer potager! We always have an abundance of beautiful fine haricots verts, or green beans, our egg basket is full, vibrant fresh radishes are regularly enjoyed, and the small colorful cherry tomatoes have begun to make their appearance in the warmth of the greenhouse. A classic and simple whole grain mustard vinaigrette is all that is needed as the perfect dressing for this salad of summer garden abundance! This vegetable platter can be made based on personal choice or from what you have on hand; the quantities are completely flexible.

SERVES 4

1 pound / 450 g fresh green beans

A few radishes and radish leaves (I love a combination of both)

10 to 12 cherry tomatoes, halved or quartered

3 or 4 farm-fresh eggs, at room temperature, boiled for about 6 minutes for semi-hard

Stems and flowers of assorted herbs, such as dill, fennel, tarragon, chervil

A handful of kalamata or violette olives

FOR THE VINAIGRETTE

2 tablespoons whole grain mustard

2 tablespoons olive oil

2 tablespoons lemon juice

1 tablespoon honey

1 small garlic clove or half of a larger clove, crushed or grated

2 sprigs of fresh tarragon, or about ½ tablespoon, chopped

Pinch of sea salt and freshly ground black pepper

Blanch the green beans by cooking in boiling water for 5 minutes then immediately shocking in an ice bath to retain color and crispness. On a large platter, begin by spreading out the green beans.

Layer the radishes, radish leaves, cherry tomatoes and cooked eggs around the platter and top with the herbs and olives.

About 30 minutes before serving, make the vinaigrette. In a small jar, combine the mustard, oil, lemon juice, honey, garlic, tarragon, and salt and pepper to taste. Serve the dressing on the side.

Orecchiette and Tuna Salad with Summer Herb Pistou

Whether you are preparing a few summer dishes to tote to a picnic or premaking delicious cold salads for summer meals, pasta salad options are always in my repertoire. I make double quantities of my favorite pastas and store them in resealable bags in the refrigerator, ready to be made into several variations of salads. This is a zesty and satisfying pasta salad that is uncomplicated and delicious. Create a bright herb-y pistou by processing all the ingredients for the pistou in a food processor or a spice blender and then toss with cooked pasta. I love the shape of orecchiette and the way its little folds hold the pistou, but you can also sub other shapes, such as macaroni or shells.

SERVES 4 TO 6

16 ounces / 450 g dried orecchiette pasta

FOR THE PISTOU

4 green onions, sliced thinly on the bias; reserve ⅓ for garnish

1 bunch of fresh basil, leaves and stems

4 sprigs of fresh oregano, leaves only

1 tablespoon lemon juice

1 tablespoon lemon zest

Pinch of salt

2 tablespoons olive oil

10 ounces / 284 g high-quality canned tuna, packed in oil

2 tablespoons capers

Cracked black pepper, for finishing

Cook the pasta according to the package instructions. After draining the pasta, rinse with cold water, drain again and set aside in a large mixing or serving bowl.

To prepare the pistou, in the bowl of a food processor, combine the green onions, basil, oregano, lemon juice and zest, salt, and oil.

Partially drain the tuna and break it into pieces. Add it to the pasta bowl and lightly toss. Add the pistou and the capers and a sprinkling of black pepper to finish. Garnish with the green onions.

Last-Minute Roasted Red Pepper Pasta Salad

This pasta salad is perfect for that last-minute picnic or BBQ invitation. It looks fancy but aside from a few fresh additions, almost all of it comes from staples you no doubt will have in your pantry with no pre-prep shopping required! This recipe works with any type of pasta, but spaghetti or linguine makes a great bed for the multiple textures of the ingredients. I use a red pepper pasta that adds both flavor and color to the dish. You can make this pasta salad in advance, leaving off the fresh oregano until just before serving. I love this recipe because the pasta salad can stay at room temperature or on an outside picnic table for a long time without any danger of the ingredients going bad. If made the day before, the flavors get even better.

SERVES 4 TO 6

16 ounces / 450 g fancy spaghetti of your choice

14 ounces / 400 g of jarred artichoke hearts, drained; reserve the liquid to dress the salad

Salt (optional)

12 ounces / 340 grams of jarred roasted peppers, drained and chopped if peppers are whole or in large pieces

6 ounces / 170 g pitted French green olives

2 cups / 400 g (about 12) halved cherry tomatoes

One bunch of arugula

Several branches of fresh oregano, or ½ tablespoon dried oregano

1 cup / 150 g crumbled feta cheese

Salt and freshly ground black pepper

Cook the pasta according to the package directions. Rinse with cold water, drain, and put in a large bowl.

Pour the marinade from the artichoke hearts over the cooked spaghetti and toss the pasta to be sure that it is evenly covered. Be sure to taste the saltiness of the marinade before adding additional salt to it. If you feel that the pasta could use a little more dressing, you can use the oil from the roasted red peppers or add olive oil.

I like using a large flat platter rather than a deep bowl to ensure that everyone gets lots of the toppings. With tongs, place the pasta on the platter and add the roasted peppers, olives, and cherry tomatoes. Top with the arugula, oregano, and feta and sprinkle with salt and pepper to taste.

Farm Stand Summer Vegetable Corn Salad

Inspired by my grandmother's garden, this bright and colorful salad encompasses everyone's favorite summer vegetables. Almost every ingredient can be found in a late-summer garden or at a farm stand: cherry tomatoes, peppers, fresh herbs, and you can easily use store-bought corn if you don't have access to corn on the cob. The corn is the base for this salad, and the rest is left up to the maker, based on the suggestions below. Add as little or as much as you have in your garden—just as my grandma did—and what you love to eat!

SERVES 6

4 cups / 700 g blanched fresh corn or organic canned corn

1 medium bulb of fennel, thinly sliced

6 to 8 radishes, sliced

1 half medium cucumber, cubed

12 cherry tomatoes, halved

¼ medium red or yellow pepper, diced (jarred or pickled work too)

1 to 2 raw banana peppers or mild green chili peppers, diced

¼ medium red onion, thinly sliced

Shaved red cabbage

FOR THE DRESSING

2 teaspoons honey

½ tablespoon red wine vinegar

¾ cup / 180 ml olive oil

1 teaspoon salt

2 tablespoons chopped fresh cilantro

1 small garlic clove, finely grated

Freshly ground black pepper

FOR THE GARNISH

3 green onions, sliced

1 bulb fennel, shaved

Handful of purple basil, chiffonaded

Handful of curly parsley, chopped

In a large salad bowl or on a large platter, assemble the corn, fennel, radishes, cucumbers, cherry tomatoes, red peppers, banana peppers, red onion, and cabbage.

To make the dressing, in a small jar, combine the honey, vinegar, oil, salt, cilantro, garlic, and black pepper. Shake well.

Toss the salad with the amount of dressing you choose at least 20 to 30 minutes before you are ready to eat so the vegetables can soak up the tangy and sweet dressing. Add the garnish right before serving. This salad will stay fresh and crunchy even when made days in advance.

pickled variation

Transform this salad into a delicious pickled vegetable garnish for burgers or cold summer soups (see page 118) by adding an additional tablespoon of vinegar before storing in the fridge.

Panna Cotta

Panna cotta has long been a recipe that I love to both make and eat! Lovely creaminess and lightly sweet, it is also versatile in the number of ways you can flavor and present it. Basic panna cotta is made with a vanilla flavor base. It takes less than 20 minutes to prepare and then about 3 hours to fully set. As a topping, you can also utilize almost any summer fruit, such as strawberries, peaches, blueberries, or raspberries.

SERVES 4 TO 6

¼ cup / 60 ml cold whole milk

1½ teaspoons powdered gelatin

2 cups / 480 ml heavy cream

¼ cup / 50 g sugar

1 vanilla bean, split, with seeds scraped with a flat knife, or ½ teaspoon vanilla extract

Fresh strawberries, soaked in Elderflower Syrup (page 95), for topping

Fresh mint or lemon verbena, for garnish

In a medium glass bowl, whisk together the milk and powder. Set aside to bloom (the gelatin powder will expand and absorb the milk) for 5 minutes.

In a medium saucepan over medium heat, combine the heavy cream, sugar, vanilla beans, and scraped seeds. Once the sugar has completely dissolved, allow the cream to come to a low boil, while stirring constantly and then immediately remove the pan from the heat. Remove the vanilla beans and then pour the hot cream mixture over the gelatin. Whisk until combined.

Spoon the panna cotta into small bowls or glasses (I love using yogurt jars) and then place the jars in the refrigerator to chill and set for 3 hours or overnight.

Prepare a bowl of halved strawberries and add ¼ cup / 60 ml of the elderflower syrup. Marinate the strawberries in the syrup while the panna cotta is setting. Layer the strawberries on top of the finished panna cotta and garnish with the mint.

Broken Rhubarb Tart

Perhaps my love affair with rhubarb began a little late in life. I recall eating strawberry rhubarb pie that my grandmother used to make and wishing it was only strawberry. It was not until much later in life that I finally embraced the vibrant tartness and lovely fragrance of this odd vegetable that is so often used as a sweet ingredient. This tart, which I designated as "broken," due to its deconstructed and casual presentation, marries creamy custard, the brilliant flavor of summer rhubarb, and the irresistible crunch of *pâte sablée* French pastry.

SERVES 4 TO 6

FOR THE CUSTARD

1 vanilla bean, split, keeping seeds intact, or ½ teaspoon vanilla extract

2½ cups / 600 ml whole milk

2 tablespoons sugar

1 tablespoon cornstarch

4 large eggs

¾ cup / 180 ml Rhubarbe Confite (page 105), for serving

1 recipe Pâte Sablée (page 19), for serving

Fresh mint or lemon verbena, for garnish

To make the custard, in a medium saucepan over medium heat, add the vanilla and milk and bring to a low boil. Once the milk begins to boil, turn off the heat and allow the vanilla to steep for 15 minutes. Remove the vanilla bean halves, rinse them off, and set them aside for future use.

In a small bowl, combine the sugar and cornstarch and whisk with the eggs. Temper the egg mixture by adding small amounts of the warm milk to the eggs, while stirring rapidly. After adding 3 to 4 tablespoons of the milk to the eggs, you will be able to add the egg mixture to the remaining milk without scrambling them. If this does happen, you can strain the custard before continuing to the final step.

Heat the combined custard mixture on low until it's thickened to the point that it clings to a spoon. The custard will continue to thicken as it cools.

In the meantime, bake the pastry on a parchment lined baking sheet in a 350°F / 180°C oven until uniformly golden and crisp, about 15 minutes.

Pour the custard into four small ramekins, then place the ramekins in the refrigerator to chill and set for 3 hours.

To serve, place about 2 tablespoons of the rhubarb confite on top of each custard. Crumble the baked pastry into large pieces and add on top. I like to make large enough pieces to dip into the custard or you can make them spoon-size. Garnish each custard with the mint.

Crème Brûlée with Blackberry Coulis

Crème brûlée has to be one of the most quintessential French desserts. I love pairing this creamy decadent dessert with semi-tart seasonal fruits like blackberries for a seasonal spin that celebrates the lush dark berry flavor against the classic vanilla tones and crackly caramelized sugar top. *(Pictured on page 146.)*

SERVES 4

FOR THE CUSTARD

2 cups / 480 ml heavy cream

2 teaspoons vanilla extract, or 1 vanilla bean, split

5 egg yolks

½ cup / 100 g sugar

2 to 3 tablespoons / 25 to 38 g sugar, for brûlée topping

Preheat the oven to 300°F / 150°C.

To make the custard, in a medium saucepan over medium heat, warm the cream and vanilla. If using a vanilla bean, remove the pods once the milk has simmered and is infused with the flavor.

While the cream is warming, in a small bowl, whisk the egg yolks with the sugar, until pale in color. Continue to heat the cream for about 5 more minutes, not allowing it to boil.

Temper the egg and sugar mixture by drizzling a small amount of the cream into the bowl with the eggs while stirring to combine. Add another spoonful of cream and combine completely, then slowly pour the warmed egg mixture into the pan of cream and vanilla. (See more on tempering on page 18.) Whisk to blend.

Prepare a deep sheet pan by making a bain-marie of water to surround the brûlée ramekins or bowls. Pour the custard into crème brûlée ramekins and bake for 50 minutes, until the custard is mainly firm and only slightly jiggly in the center.

Place the ramekins in the refrigerator to chill for a minimum of 30 minutes. You can also suspend the preparation of the crème brûlée to serve later or on the following day by leaving in the fridge, covered with a dish towel, and only adding the sugar and torching it right before presentation.

To caramelize the sugar, sprinkle a thick layer of sugar on top of each custard and, using a torch, move the flame uniformly across the surface until a golden bubbly crust forms. You can also brûlée the dessert under the broiler in a pinch; however, it is more difficult to achieve a consistent result with this method without the risk of burning.

FOR THE COULIS

10 ounces / 280 g (just over 1 cup) fresh blackberries

Juice of ½ lemon (about 1 tablespoon)

⅓ cup / 65 g sugar

Fresh blackberries, for garnish

Fresh mint or lemon verbena, for garnish

To make the coulis, in a small saucepan over medium-low heat, warm the blackberries, lemon juice, and sugar. Stir to dissolve the sugar and simmer for 10 to 15 minutes, until it becomes slightly thickened.

Remove the pan from the heat and pour the mixture through a fine-mesh strainer to remove the seeds. Chill until ready to use.

To serve, place one spoonful of the coulis on each custard after the sugar has brûléed. Garnish with fresh blackberries and mint.

Fruit Salad with Elderflower Granita

Often in the summer, the need for dessert falls to the wayside. Meals are lighter, and a very cold glass of rosé can be a perfect finish to a meal. But it is hard to refuse a vibrant cup of fruit with an icy granita, especially one made with luxuriously floral and fragrant elderflowers. Use your favorite summer fruits, such as blueberries, strawberries, blackberries, peaches, or nectarines in any quantity or combination.

SERVES 4

2 cups / 480 ml Elderflower Syrup (page 95)

1 ⅓ cup / 220 g strawberries, tops removed, quartered

1 cup / 170 g blueberries

½ cup / 80 g blackberries

2 passion fruits, with pulp and seeds

1 cup / 150 g cantaloupe or honeydew melon, diced

2 white nectarines or peaches, diced

Fresh mint, basil, or lemon balm, for garnish

Pour the elderflower syrup into a deep sheet pan and place the pan in the freezer for a minimum of 2 hours. (I do this in the morning if we are serving guests in the evening.)

In a large bowl, combine the fruit. Fill four serving glasses with the fruit.

When ready to serve, take the pan of frozen elderflower syrup from the freezer. Use a large fork to scrape the surface, making large flakes. Spoon the granita on top of each glass of fruit. Garnish with the herbs and serve immediately.

a summer apéro

The French word *apéritif* comes from a Latin verb, meaning "to open," and, in general terms, it is a drink and a light snack to open the palate before the evening meal. Normally, this occurs an hour or more before dinner, or if it is *un apéritif dînatoire*, it is served in place of dinner, with a full selection of dishes, such as small quiches, savory cakes, and flatbreads with spreads. Or it might include a *pissaladière*, a flatbread with toppings, a *rillette,* a meat spread, or a pâté served with tiny cornichons.

The basic premise of the aperitif is that adults drink simple cocktails, wine, or aperitif liqueurs served over ice and not complicated or heavy mixed drinks. Often there is only the choice of champagne or rosé in the summertime or a glass of pastis. Children are offered bubbly water or *limonade*, made with flavored syrups, such as grenadine, lemon, or mint. This drink is called a *diablo*, *jus de pomme*, or *jus d'orange*.

The variations of food served for the aperitif are many. From a simple bowl of chips or salted nuts to a cheese platter with charcuterie, small savory pastries, and crudités. The setup or table for the aperitif also varies from casual to elegant and formal. I have been to *l'heure de l'apéro*, where a coffee table has been cleared, a bottle is passed, and a bowl of potato chips and a cutting board of *saucisson*, or dried sausage, is shared. I have also been to the same type but more formal event, where tables were covered with linen cloths and set with crystal stemware, China plates, and cloth napkins. Somewhere in the middle are those held in outdoor settings, my favorite type of aperitif.

I have found after many years of living in France that *apéro* is a lovely way to stay connected with friends, who might be too busy to accept a full dinner invitation or are not available for a long evening. Although I have hosted and attended many aperitifs, where eating and nibbling continues through the dinner hour, even if someone had already stated, "Oh, I can only stay for aperitif." I am frequently guilty of preparing a full five-course meal under the guise of being just appetizers. I suppose I can't help it that I love to feed people large amounts of food, and that my passion is creating menus from start to finish, even casual ones. I also adore the vibe of an aperitif. The mood is always light, and appetites are definitely open. If everyone is staying on for dinner, then setting a table outside or in the dining room allows me to shoo everyone out of the kitchen so I can carry on with the other preparations.

In my mind, a thoughtfully laid out aperitif not only feels welcoming, but it also gives a little preview of the deliciousness that is coming: warmed olives; salty nuts; fresh bite-size cold veggies; a fancy little pastry like *palmiers*; *gougères*, little savory cheese puffs; or a gourmet smoked sausage or salmon. And always, there are the cold drinks, ice at the ready, and the ability to improvise and create something interesting to drink even for nondrinkers.

I think you might agree that the French are masters of making a small practice or tradition into something special. There is such elegance in the simplicity of a French aperitif: a crisp white cloth, perhaps vintage glassware, silver forks, and cheese knives. There may be whole pieces of fruit freshly washed and simply laid on a plate. In the summer, adding a confiture jar with colorful blooms and maybe just a single taper candle in a brass candlestick adds a festive note. Crowding around a small table and reaching for a pinch of olives or a cherry tomato brings everyone together to celebrate a day passed and the evening to come.

Palmiers au Chorizo

Palmiers are palm-shaped pastries made with puff pastry or *pâte feuilletée*. Normally made as a sweet treat with the simple addition of sugar, the savory version will often show up on aperitif tables as a crunchy savory appetizer. If you are adventurous, try making the *pâte feuilletée* at home; otherwise, there is no shame in purchasing a high-quality store-bought version.

MAKES ABOUT 12 PASTRIES

1 (8-ounce / 230 g) sheet puff pastry (*pâte feuilletée*), thawed if frozen

1 cup / 180 g dried sliced chorizo or spicy dried salami

¼ cup / 30 g grated Parmesan cheese

Fleur de sel

Herb cheese, for serving (see below; optional)

On a large piece of parchment paper, roll out the sheet of puff pastry.

In a small food processor, add the chorizo and process until it takes on the texture of a coarse paste. Spread the paste evenly across the puff pastry and sprinkle uniformly with the Parmesan. Roll the long edge of the pastry as tightly as possible, until you reach the center of the sheet and then do the same on the other side so that both "rolls" meet. Wrap the parchment paper around the rolled pastry and return the pastry to the refrigerator to chill for 30 minutes. If you want to stop here and make the finished pastry just before your guests arrive, the pastry can be held in the refrigerator overnight and cut the following day just before baking.

Preheat the oven to 425°F / 220°C. Line a sheet pan with parchment paper.

To make the *palmiers*, unroll the parchment paper on a cutting board and slice the roll, gently holding the two sides together and reshaping slightly as needed. Each slice should be about 1½ inches / 4 cm thick. Place each piece 2 to 3 inches / 5 to 7.5 cm apart on the prepared pan and bake for 12 to 15 minutes. Sprinkle with fleur de sel to finish.

Chorizo *palmiers* are delicious on their own and are even more delicious spread with the herb cheese.

Herb Cheese

Combine ½ cup / 120 g traditional spreadable cream cheese with equal parts soft goat cheese. Add 1 tablespoon each of chopped fresh chives, dill, parsley, and dried shallots. Add ½ cup / 120 g sour cream and salt to taste.

Eggplant Tapenade

A perfect summery vegetable spread where the eggplants are the star. I have simplified the methods for making a traditional tapenade by doing a one-pan version of summer vegetables, coarsely chopped, and then blended for a rustic and delicious tapenade to spread on toast or slices of baguette or flat bread. Classically, a tapenade was used as a sauce or a topping for meats or seafood, and it was the French that influenced the use of tapenade as a spread for bread.

SERVES 4 TO 6

2 medium eggplants, cut into cubes

1 red onion, diced

½ cup / 80 g chopped red bell peppers

¼ cup / 60 ml olive oil

2 cups / 400 g fresh tomatoes, about 3 medium tomatoes, diced

2 tablespoons capers

8 to 10 large pitted green olives

8 to 10 pitted black olives

½ cup / 120 ml red wine vinegar

Sea salt and freshly ground black pepper

Place the eggplant on a large sheet pan. Add the onion and bell peppers and toss with the oil, then add the tomatoes, capers, and both kinds of olives.

Preheat the oven to 200°F / 90°C.

Place the pan with the vegetables in the oven and roast for 20 to 25 minutes.

Remove the pan from the oven and add the roasted vegetables to a food processor. Pulse to the desired consistency, while adding the vinegar. Season with salt and pepper to taste.

variations

For an added punch, add a teaspoon of chili flakes or a few fillets of anchovies or sardines for rich saltiness.

You can also sub balsamic vinegar in place of the red wine vinegar for extra sweetness.

making hay

After several summers at Rabbit Hill, we began to feel settled into farm life. Our adventure had begun with our rooster and hens and had moved forward not only with the addition of the goats but soon after, with the gift of a little black lamb. Life was full. We had arranged to rent a small parcel of extra land around the house for animal grazing, and we had started the lavender field. In the evenings we toted folding chairs to the grassy areas to sit and watch the chickens stroll by or to hold a baby goat on our laps. Our children explored, wandering beyond the fence lines, bringing back handfuls of acorns, twigs, and interesting rocks. We mowed only a small patch for seating or for the placement of a small wading pool for hot summer days and, yes, even the essential part of every childhood summer, the brightly colored Slip 'N Slide.

Several times a year we received small deliveries of hay. We purchased only enough to line the barn stalls and chicken coop and to feed the few goats and single sheep that we had at the time. I remember when we received our first hay delivery. A young friend with an ancient tractor that squeaked and creaked drove up our gravel driveway and deposited neatly cubed bales of golden stalks and stems. I remember feeling that now it was official—we had a farm.

But none of that could match the feeling of the summer we made hay. Following a significantly wet spring and a sunny, warm summer, the lower field was almost waist high and filled with the perfect mélange of weeds, wildflowers, and grasses. For fun and adventure, we had mowed a grid of pathways throughout the hay field that allowed our cats to wander and stalk small mice and our daughter to pick blooms or play hide-and-seek. By late summer, the tall grasses had become dry, and seeds had dispersed and settled to renew the "prairie" next season.

I am not sure how we came to decide to make hay. It might have been a comment made by that same young farmer who had delivered the hay, that our pasture was good enough to make hay. So, one evening after a long, hot day, the little red tractor returned, pulling the required machinery to cut the field and to lay out long rows ready for the baler. We were sitting at the dinner table when he arrived, and we quickly set our glasses down and left our plates of food. I, of course, ran to get my camera. It felt akin to what vineyards must feel like on harvest day—exciting and festive, even if it was only humble hay.

For the best hay, a variety of elements must fall into place. Although the most nutritious hay

comes from a field before it flowers, it is still valuable after flowering. Most importantly, the hay must be completely dry and then baled and stored immediately. That particular summer, we waited for a window between rain showers with enough dry days to ensure a good harvest.

Hundreds of years ago, it could take weeks to harvest and store hay, when almost the entire process was done by hand or with simple mechanical means. The expression "making hay" represents the proverb of taking the opportunity when the conditions are right. Sometimes making hay is a waiting game of timing, sun, and clear skies . . . or just timing it right between storms.

There are many lessons in making hay. From taking something that can easily be wasted, like weeds, wildflowers, and grasses, and making something useful with it. Pastures that seasonally grow to be used for hay are left to flourish, unattended until harvest day. There is a lesson also in honoring something that is humble: harvesting and storing hay correctly and ultimately providing nutrition to livestock. Some farms are made and broken by a successful or failed hay harvest.

Why is it that something as simple as making hay for our farm feels so magical? The memory of it brings comfort and calmness and a sense of fulfillment. What fun to watch our kids (and dogs) chase the tractor. We love to sit on the hay bales, feeling the dry breezes. As we stand on tall ladders and lift the bales to the loft, we savor the sweet smell of the fresh hay. Listening to the seasons, we prepare for the future.

AUTUMN

L' AUTOMNE

AUTUMN HAS ALWAYS HELD a special place in my heart. Even before Rabbit Hill, the season was made special by my birthday celebration and fall travel plans. If the summer extends into fall, giving us warmer days, I impatiently await that first chill in the air. Sometimes Normandy stays mild well into November, but it is the arrival of the beautiful light, as it extends in long shadows across the kitchen, that always signals the change of season. The copper pots and pans hanging on the racks cast reflections of warm light. We light candles in the early evening, and when it's finally cool enough, we make a fire in the living room.

Having a farm has brought a new emphasis to fall. If the dahlias were planted late or just took their time to appear, it's in the fall that they make their stunning show of dinner-plate-size blooms. It's when we peek among the squash vines to see if we have new pumpkins, or if there will be enough round, hot orange-hued potimarron squash to make soup through the winter. Occasionally, the green beans and eggplants will push through to the end of October, surprising us with late harvests.

Before the gales and rain come, I cut back the mint and verbena to dry and store to make tisane. We pick the last of the peppers and watch them as they change from a deep green to a hot vibrant red and, with patience, they will become dry enough to grind into a hot, aromatic chili powder. We dry and smoke the Espelette and paprika peppers, store them in airtight jars to add to dishes for just the right touch of flavor.

Fall is also time to collect seeds. I learned the importance of doing this after several growing seasons. Once the tomato vines have begun to go brown and dry, the remaining tomatoes will fall and become the seedlings for the following summer. The best tomatoes are from season after season of volunteer plants. Heirloom tomatoes are always stronger plants which yield tastier fruits. The only work involved is thinning the baby plants in the hope that you are preserving the best variety. We collect bean pods and put them in mesh bags to dry, until there is time to crack them open and reserve the smooth, shiny seeds. We gather sunflower seeds and dry them before the birds and mice make a feast of them.

If the change of light or slight chill in the air are not enough to signal the change of the seasons, then the livestock on the farm provide a distinct cue. The donkeys and goats have their second heat season of the year. The chickens go into a rest mode and molt, shedding their old feathers, which will be replaced with new fluffy down. During seasonal molting, hens and roosters often drop weight and have less energy, and often cease egg production. If you are lucky, the hens will molt at different times, so egg collection will drop, but not stop altogether. When our ducks and geese molt, it's less noticeable, as their closely packed, dense feathers protect their skin, and they rarely develop the bald patches that we see in the chickens. What we do see are the lovely long wing feathers of the geese scattered around the barnyard that our daughter sometimes brings into the house for a spontaneous art project.

In mid-autumn, we say goodbye to our neighbor's cows, who appear each spring in the fields next to the house. We love having them there—such fascinating creatures. In our first years at Rabbit Hill, there were sometimes up to two dozen Normandy cows with only a simple fence between them and the kitchen windows. Dairy cows are quite docile and even friendly. When my daughter was very young, she would crawl under the fence, and we would often find her nose to nose with one of cows. We soon nicknamed her the cow whisperer.

The flavors of autumn in my kitchen are aromatic and sweet. Meats are slowly cooked to the point of being fork-tender. My heavy cast-iron Dutch oven is always within arm's reach. A basket of taper candles is at the ready, as brass candlesticks stand aglow each evening, while dinner preparations commence.

autumn in belle normandy

Autumn in Normandy is magnificent. Temperatures still tease from summer, the cloudless skies shine brilliant low light, and the sunsets are stunningly vibrant. Autumn is often the time when we advise people to visit and never once has a guest regretted the tip.

Normandy also offers the perfect marriage of forest and sea. So, there is no question why it leads in the culinary category of *Cuisine du Terroir*. The word *terroir* derives from the Latin term that defines land (location) and terrain (dirt). In the kitchen, this means that the dishes that are created honor local ancient traditions in combination with the climate and attributes of the region. *Cuisine du Terroir* promotes the intimate relationship between the kitchen and the soil and the ingredients that are either grown or found, farmed, or foraged. Honoring the local gastronomy and culture, it utilizes age-old methods from preparation to presentation.

Local restaurants in the region continue to honor this tradition, which has seen a resurgence in popularity over the last decade with the farm-to-table movement and the push to support local producers. We know many multigenerational farmers who live close by and chefs that stay true to the cooking methods of the cooks who came before them. Normandy cuisine highlights regional specialties, from local fish and seafood to farm-raised poultry, beef and pork to organ meats, rabbits, and wild fowl. Apples and, of course, cider and Calvados, along with a wide variety of cheeses, find their way into almost all the dishes.

I began my true immersion into *Cuisine Normande* before finding our home at Rabbit Hill. My father-in-law was a classically trained chef, and his influence on my cooking is something I am forever grateful for, since it was cooking that connected me to my French family. Meal by meal, I believe I won over their hearts. For my in-laws, I became more than just the American girl who was able to settle their youngest wayfaring son or the one who finally convinced him to return to his roots and to his hometown. I became the woman who would go to all ends to please them and show my commitment to making a go of it here.

My father-in-law, Jean, met my husband's mother, Janine, in Trouville-sur-Mer in 1952. At the time, he was eighteen years old and was completing an internship at a local hotel as part of his education as a hotel manager and chef for the *Ecole Hôtelière de Paris*. Janine was sixteen years old and working at her mother's hotel restaurant on rue Carnot. A chance meeting at a local beachside dance hall led to their long future together in running the family restaurant called Carmen, named after the opera by George Bizet. The villa that became the location for Carmen had been owned by the Bizet family in the late 19th century. After several years of working in Paris to finish his education and a two-year period serving as an officer in the French Army, Jean returned to marry Janine in 1957 and took over the responsibilities of running Carmen soon after. Four children and thirty-eight years later, they officially retired and handed over the restaurant to my husband's older brother, who had also trained as a professional chef. Almost all of this predates me. In fact, it was the year that we married when my husband's parents, whom we call Manou and Papi, stepped away from Carmen.

I first met my in-laws only two days before I married their son. They had traveled from Normandy to West Los Angeles, California, to attend our wedding, which was held in an intimate glass-walled chapel on a hillside in Palos Verdes. They knew only a little about me, and I knew even less about them. The date of our wedding was planned around their ability to take vacation time, which they barely ever did, and fly a very long distance to witness our vows and to meet my parents and family for the first time as well. I loved them. Of course, I did. And there was something about Papi—the way he did the *bise*, the double cheek kiss upon greeting, three times instead of just two; how he thoughtfully regarded the large platters of food that were served at the American restaurants and found a compliment for every dish he tried, even though he was a far better cook; the way he squeezed my hand to let me know I had passed the very quick test and approval to marry his son.

Four years later, after we had our first son, who was nine months old, we traveled to France to meet the rest of my husband's family. I was wined and dined, the advantage of having two professional chefs in the immediate family. There were gatherings around long tables and long lunches. I will never forget how hard it was to stay attentive during a three-hour lunch while slightly jet-lagged and sleep deprived as the mother of a young baby. I soon realized that I barely understood a single word and hoped that an additional glass of wine might open up the language part of my brain. I also recognized for the first time how different our two worlds were, the American to the French, and how that would change the rest of my life.

When we moved to France, it was just after our fifteenth wedding anniversary. After living in the United States as a couple for sixteen years and having only visited France three times, our expectations were high. We would integrate seamlessly into our French family. I would learn the language and fully embrace the culture and leave behind, without regret, a life that had been familiar to me for more than forty years. How much of that came true?

Maybe God has a different story for you. That was my thought almost a decade later. For me, he did. Becoming part of a new family in an unfamiliar culture would be a long and sometimes complicated endeavor. Learning the language, beyond becoming astute at culinary vocabulary and terms, turned out to

be far more difficult. This came as a surprise to me since I had always accomplished every goal in every self-taught effort. Leaving behind a predictable lifestyle and supportive friends turned out to be my greatest challenge. Continual issues with immigration that made me feel that France wasn't embracing me as much as I was embracing it also became an issue. And then there was the language barrier that stood between me and my ability to make new friends and to be fully accepted by our French family.

But for some reason, I never struggled in communicating or bonding with Papi. Our common love language of food and feeding people sealed the gap that might otherwise have been occupied with words. In those first

years, I would subtly take notes on everything he cooked for family celebrations or casual meals. I would ask questions and observe. Once we had the ability to host at Rabbit Hill, with our well-equipped, light-filled kitchen and large dining room, we invited family as often as possible. There were countless Sunday lunches and holidays; Easter and Thanksgiving were my favorites. When Papi arrived at our home, he would enter the kitchen and lift pot lids and peruse the countertop and make comments about my mise en place, the process in which ingredients are prepared and organized. I might exit the kitchen and bring him a spoon of sauce to try, while everyone was relaxing in the living room before a meal. During the lunch, he would smile and nod, sometimes getting lost in the moment, enjoying a dish that I had made, while tapping his fingers on the table, keeping beat with the soft jazz music playing in the background.

In the years since his passing, I have had to forgive myself for not asking more questions. I wish I had mastered French well enough to have had long conversations. I would have asked about his life as a culinary student, about his favorite thing to eat at the end of a long service or on days off, and for the secret to his stock. And I certainly would have asked him what he considered to be his biggest accomplishment. I am pretty sure he would have said it was his family.

Instead of the answers to those questions, he will be remembered for the dedication that he modeled and the love that he gave. For some family members, he is remembered for his stunning mayonnaise that he whisked expertly with a fork or for his Sunday lamb roast. For others, it is for how he made his *escargots Janine*, which were escargots prepared with garlic and

parsley butter in special individual ramekin dishes that he made especially for my mother-in-law, who didn't like escargots served in their shells. And, finally, there is his love of jazz music and an evening whiskey.

I still remember the day that while visiting us in Marin County, he set out for a short walk in the early morning and didn't return until early evening. He was always eager to explore and learn more, but in the days before cell phones, it certainly made us worry. I well remember how he could put together a simple platter of cheese and a perfectly dressed salad and make it seem like a feast on a Sunday evening. I recall a time when I was facing a particularly difficult situation, he took my hand firmly and said a single word that healed all worry—*courage*, a word that happens to be the same in both English and French. When I made something traditional but added my own twist, he would give me the highest compliment: *"C'est originale!"* This was his way of saying, *"C'est magnifique!"* I will always remember that from the first day we met, he believed in me and in everything I set out to do.

So often when I make a dish or a sauce that he loved (and he was quite passionate about sauces!), I think of him. There is an armchair in our dining room that we found at a flea market specifically for him to sit at a place of honor when we purchased a larger dining table. Recently on a cold autumn afternoon, I reached in the back of an armoire for a sweater and realized it was his. And perhaps most significantly, his beloved collection of copper cookware hangs from my pot rack as a reminder of his unconditional love of family. I often sense that the walls of my kitchen still hold his spirit, and I am certain that he is still cheering me on.

slow-cooking sundays

Autumn brings the return of slow-cooking Sundays, a long-standing practice in our home that originated during our first fall season at Rabbit Hill. During the spring and summer months, our weekends are taken up by flea markets and vintage sales, and we catch lunch on the go (very un-French, but acceptable if you are going to a flea market) often of *saucisse-frites*, which is a barbecued chipolata or merguez sausage and a small basket of fries that is eaten at a picnic table between hours of strolling the tables on the hunt for good finds. But in the fall, when the last markets wrap up until the following spring, I am back in the kitchen creating something that will stew for hours, becoming decadently rich and extraordinarily tender and delicious.

I'm not shy about my love for the humble Dutch oven. It's not fancy, and the cooking you do with it is not haute cuisine. Called a cocotte in both English and French, these pots were made for hearth cooking and braising over low heat for extended periods of time. (They are named after the Dutch, when they mastered the required casting techniques to make the pots sturdy but less expensive.) Most are still made of cast-iron and have a protective enamel finish, and if not, are still made with a substantially thick bottom that promotes stewing instead of the rapid transfer of heat. In modern kitchens, attempts have been made to replace them with electric slow cookers but ask any foodie, and they will agree that searing is a necessary first step in any good braise, and this has yet to be perfected in convenient appliances.

My Dutch oven rarely sees the inside of a cupboard during the cooler months, and the ritual of slow cooking on a Sunday is one that we have grown to cherish. Slowing down for us is always a challenge. Farm life is inherently busy, and there is never an end to the constant tasks and chores. But on Sundays, we force ourselves for at least part of the day, to focus on family and rest. Beyond the undisturbed cooking that is required, nothing evokes a cozier and slower day than setting a timer and heading to a comfortable chair with a cup of tea and a book, while your lunch cooks to perfection. For one-pot cooking, most of the effort is spent creating the mise en place, setting up the dish and then cleaning up after putting it into the oven. Then you can be free, at least for a few hours.

Sunday is the busiest day of the week for local boulangeries, since Sunday lunch is the most significant meal of the week. The long lines start early in the morning. People are not only getting the bread for lunch and dinner but are also buying a pastry or fancy dessert because no one is on a diet on Sundays! Leftover bread is always saved for a light dinner of cheese and salad and maybe a small cup of soup. Any excess bread after that will become Monday morning tartines.

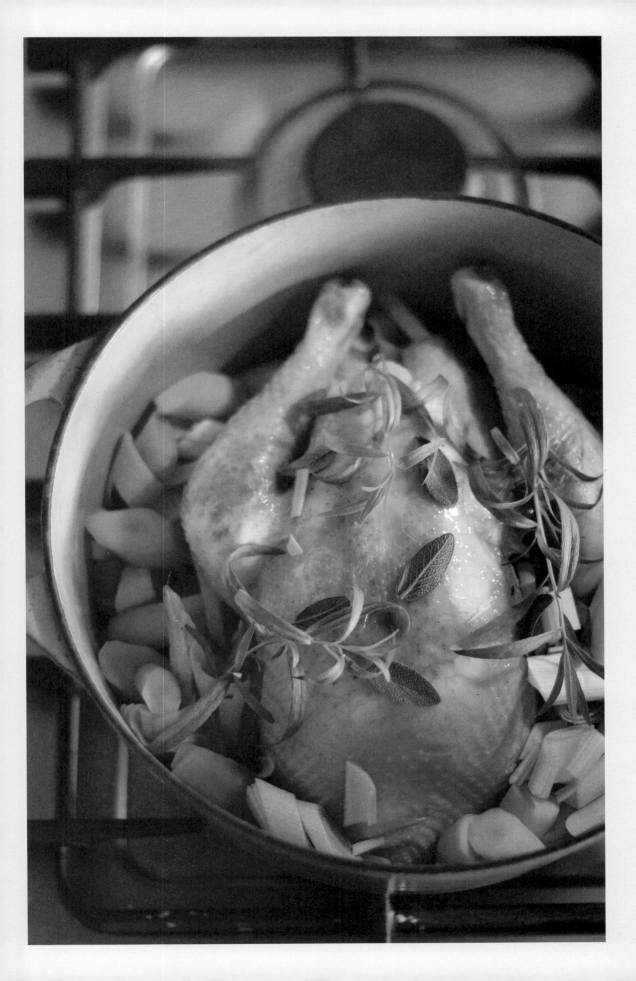

Huîtres Gratinées

Broiled Oysters with Pesto Butter

Although oysters are available throughout France, Normandy and Brittany are famed for theirs, with consumption dating back to hundreds of thousands of years. From roadside vending machines (yes, there are!) to Michelin Star menus, fresh oysters are enjoyed mainly from September to January. Often simply served raw on the half shell with a lemon wedge or vinegar-based mignonette, a popular and gourmet preparation can be made by making oysters broiled au gratin. This is a great way to introduce oysters to hesitant tasters, and I think this recipe will win them over!

SERVES 6 AS AN APPETIZER

2 dozen fresh oysters

2 tablespoons unsalted butter, cut into small pats, 1 per oyster shell

¼ cup / 60 ml store-bought pesto

Crusty bread, for serving

Clean the oysters by scrubbing the shells with a stiff vegetable brush to remove any seaweed or grit on the exterior. Shuck the oysters (pry them open with an oyster knife or blunt knife) and drain. This is done by gently tipping the oyster and letting any liquid drip out. Keep in mind that oysters will continue to release water, so you may have to drain them several times before broiling. It's always a good idea to test an oyster for saltiness. If you find they are too salty due to the seawater, rinse them (holding the half shell and oyster under running tap water). They should be fresh and taste and smell like the ocean.

Preheat the broiler.

In a large roasting pan or sheet pan, place the half shell oysters, doing your best to prop them upright. This can also be achieved by lining your pan with a bed of course salt. Place a pat of butter and ½ teaspoon of the pesto on each oyster.

Broil for 2 to 3 minutes or until the pesto begins to brown and the butter is melted.

Serve immediately with small slices of crusty bread to catch the delicious melted butter and pesto. We often find ourselves standing at the counter with a napkin in hand and eating the oysters right from the pan. As a serving suggestion, a lovely small glass of Sauternes wine is the perfect complement to the salty and buttery oysters.

Salt-Cured Duck Breast

Autumn is duck season, and my love of locally farmed duck manifests itself in so many recipes! This one has an air of elegance, yet it is simple and rustic. Salt-drying meat was derived by necessity as one of the oldest methods of preserving food. Once cured, duck breast can be used for up to one year but is best used within six months. In thin slices, it is a beautiful and delicious addition to a charcuterie or cheese board, and shaved, it becomes a gourmet topping for risotto or pasta dishes.

**MAKES 1 CURED
DUCK BREAST**

2 pounds / 900 g coarse white sea salt or kosher salt

1 (18 to 24-ounce / 510 to 680 g) duck breast

2 tablespoons herbes de Provence

Cracked black pepper

In a shallow glass casserole dish, lay a bed of salt about 2 inches / 5 cm thick. Lay the duck breast on top and then cover with the remaining salt. The entire duck breast should be concealed in the salt. Cover the dish and place in the refrigerator for 24 to 48 hours. There is a variance of time, based on the size of the duck breast. To test, brush off some of the salt and poke the breast with your finger; it should have lost a significant amount of moisture and not feel tender any longer.

Remove the breast from the dish and brush off the salt. Discard the salt and lay the breast on a large sheet of parchment paper. Rub the skin and meat with the herbes de Provence and add the desired amount of black pepper to both sides.

Wrap the parchment paper loosely around the breast and then roll in a clean towel. Tie with a piece of butcher's string and put the bundle into the refrigerator to cure for 3 weeks.

The duck breast can remain wrapped in the parchment and towel but does need to be put in a different container between uses. It's best for it to remain as dry as possible. Allow duck breast slices to come to room temperature before serving.

Quiche aux Légumes — Vegetable Quiche

Time and again, a simple quiche saves lunchtime during a busy week on the farm. Making a quiche is a great way to utilize random vegetables and excess eggs when the chickens are producing almost dozens a day in the early autumn. There are endless vegetable combinations that work, and nothing needs to be fancy or measured precisely. Just fresh eggs, a variety of additions and a good pastry to bring it together. I love the combination of sautéed cabbage, leeks, and potatoes, accented by a topping of strips of smoky bacon. It is quick to make if you have a store-bought pastry on hand that is already thawed, and it stores well and reheats beautifully!

SERVES 6

1 recipe *pâte brisée* pastry (page 19) or store-bought pastry, thawed

6 eggs

1 teaspoon Dijon mustard

1 tablespoon butter

1 tablespoon olive oil

¼ green cabbage, roughly sliced into thin pieces

3 medium leeks, washed and diced

1 cup / 150 grams cooked potatoes, diced

4 thick-cut bacon strips for the top

On a lightly floured surface, roll the pastry into a 10-inch / 25 cm diameter circle, and fit the pastry round into an 8-inch / 20 cm diameter tart pan. Fold over the edges and crimp if there is excess. Put the pastry in the tart pan into the refrigerator to chill while you prepare the quiche filling. Preheat the oven to 325°F / 160°C.

In a large bowl, whisk the eggs with the mustard. In a medium sauté pan, add the butter and oil. Once the butter is melted, add the cabbage and leeks and cooked potatoes. Sauté for about 5 minutes, or until tender. Place the vegetables on the pastry crust in a single layer, spreading evenly to the edges. Fill with the egg mixture and then lay the strips of smoked bacon on top.

Bake for 30 minutes or until the bacon is fully cooked and the quiche is golden and firm in the center. Cool for 10 minutes before cutting and serving.

The quiche can be kept in the refrigerator for up to 5 days, and frozen vacuum-sealed or in a freezer container for 6 months.

Soupe aux Panais et aux Châtaignes

Parsnip Soup with Brown Butter Chestnuts

In the same family as carrots and parsley, parsnips have an earthy and aromatic sweetness that adds a distinct fall flavor to soups and stews. Roasting them enhances their natural flavor and sweetness. This soup is creamy perfection accented by buttery chestnuts, another autumn and winter staple in French homes.

Brown butter, or *beurre noisette*, is basically regular butter that is gently melted and cooked until it browns, resulting in a change of flavor, aroma, and color. There is a fine line between brown and burnt; burnt butter will have an off smell and leave an acrid taste in the mouth. My advice is to take it slowly and watch the butter as it is melting.

In France, prepared (peeled and roasted) chestnuts can be found year-round at the grocery store. They are not to be confused with candied chestnuts that are boiled in sugar syrup and are available at the markets during the holidays.

SERVES 8 AS AN APPETIZER OR 4 TO 6 AS A LUNCH

4 to 6 parsnips, cut into 2-inch / 5 cm pieces

2 cups / 340 g butternut squash, cubed

Olive oil

¼ cup / 60 g salted butter

3 shallots, finely diced

1 (14-ounce / 400 g) jar whole roasted chestnuts, sliced; reserve 6 for garnish

4 cups / 960 ml vegetable or chicken stock

Salt and freshly ground black pepper

Pinch of nutmeg

1½ cups / 360 ml heavy cream

Preheat the oven to 425°F / 220°C.

On a large sheet pan, arrange the parsnip and squash pieces in a single layer. Drizzle with the oil and roast for 20 minutes. Remove the pan from the oven and scrape the parsnip and squash pieces into a large soup pot. Add 2 tablespoons of the butter and the shallots. Cook over low heat for 5 minutes or until the shallots are tender. Add the chestnuts (remember to hold aside 6 for garnish) and simmer for 10 minutes.

Add the stock and then continue to simmer for 1 hour. Use an immersion blender to blend the soup to a smooth purée and then taste and season with salt and pepper. Add the nutmeg and cream.

To prepare the chestnuts for garnish, set a small sauté pan over low heat and add the remaining 2 tablespoons butter. Heat the butter slowly, whisking and swirling the pan to encourage even browning and keep any solids from burning. You're looking for a golden-brown hue. Just as the butter begins to brown around the edges of the pan, quickly add the chestnuts. Add sea salt to taste.

To serve, ladle the soup into deep bowls, add a few of the brown-butter chestnuts and a drizzle of brown butter on top.

Soupe de Céleri Rave — Creamy Celery Root Soup

Widely used in French cooking, *céleri-rave*, or celeriac, has a subtle celerylike flavor. Harvested in late fall and winter, it appears at the markets in November, and because of its long storage life (about eight months in the refrigerator), it is available fresh almost year-round. I use it puréed, as a stand-in for mashed potatoes, and to thicken silky soups. It can be served as a vegetarian dish with buttered croutons, or for a heartier version, I add lardons or smoked bacon.

SERVES 4

1½ pounds / 680 g celeriac (1 or 2 medium)

¼ cup / 60 g of salted butter

1 onion, finely diced

1 leek, finely chopped

4 cups / 960 ml vegetable stock

½ cup / 120 ml crème fraîche

FOR THE GARNISH

½ cup / 100 g lardons or thick-cut smoked bacon, diced

1 tablespoon butter

4 slices whole wheat bread, cut into 1-inch / 2.5 cm cubes

Crème fraîche, for topping

Salt and white pepper

Using a sharp knife, remove both ends of the celeriac, then use a potato peeler to remove the tough skin. Rinse if needed and cut into small dices.

In a large soup pot over medium-high heat, add the butter and heat until melted. Add the onion and leek and cook until tender, about 5 minutes. Reserve about ¼ cup for the garnish and set aside. Turn down the heat to medium and add the celeriac. Continue to sauté until the cubes begin to become tender.

Add the stock and simmer for 30 minutes. Use an immersion blender to purée until smooth, then add the crème fraîche.

To prepare the garnish, in a large sauté pan, cook the lardons until brown and crispy, then add the butter. Once the butter has melted, toss the cubes of bread into the pan and sauté until evenly golden.

To serve, top the soup with a spoonful of crème fraîche and garnish with the lardon mixture. Add salt and pepper to taste.

Camembert aux Pommes

Baked Camembert with Apples

Camembert is a cow's milk cheese similar to Brie, but it has a slightly stronger taste. Occasionally tangy, it can be slightly nutty and is quite buttery. In France, Camembert is made with raw milk that is salted and then ripened, creating a soft outer skin or rind. When heated, it melts to a lush creamy texture. It pairs perfectly with tart apples and honey in this easy and popular appetizer. If you can find Camembert in its traditional round box or wood crate, you can bake it directly in its carton once you have removed the paper or plastic that it is wrapped in. Be sure to have plenty of baguette pieces to dip into the delicious creaminess.

**SERVES 2 TO 4 AS
AN APPETIZER**

1 Granny Smith apple, skin on, cut into thin matchsticks

2 teaspoons lemon juice

1 teaspoon sugar

1 (9-ounce / 250 g) round Camembert cheese

3 tablespoons / 64 g honey

2 or 3 sprigs of fresh thyme, or 1 tablespoon dried thyme

Fleur de sel, for finishing

Baguette slices, for serving

In a small bowl, mix the apple, lemon juice, and sugar together and set aside.

Remove the Camembert from its box, unwrap it, and place it back in the box. If your cheese does not come in a carton, remove the wrapping and place it in a small round baking or gratin dish. There is no need to remove the natural "skin" or rind of the cheese.

Score the top of the cheese by cutting diagonal slashes through the surface with a knife. This opens the rind and allows the honey and herbs to seep in as the cheese melts. Top with the apple and drizzle with half of the honey.

Preheat the oven to 325°F / 160°C.

Place the cheese, in its carton, on a sheet pan and bake for 10 minutes.

Remove the pan from the oven and drizzle with the remaining honey and top with the thyme. Finish with a sprinkle of fleur de sel and serve with soft baguette slices.

Folded Wild Mushroom Omelet

Our nephew is a mycophile (someone who hunts for wild, edible mushrooms), and on one cold, wet autumn day, he arrived in our kitchen with crates of foraged mushrooms. After an impromptu lesson, I was excited to hone my mushroom-searing skills, and my mouth watered when I saw the large amount of girolles (commonly called chanterelles). I envisioned soups and cream sauces, but in my eagerness to taste them, I grabbed a few eggs and set out to make a simple omelet. Eggs complement the subtle mushroom flavors perfectly and are the star of this simple dish that can be eaten as a brunch dish or a casual dinner.

SERVES 2

8 ounces / 225 g mixed wild mushrooms

¼ cup / 60 g salted butter

Drizzle of olive oil

2 medium shallots, diced

6 medium eggs

Cold water, for beating the eggs

Salt and freshly ground black pepper

1 tablespoon chopped fresh parsley

Clean and dry the mushrooms using a damp cloth or a brush, since sometimes wild mushrooms already have a good amount of moisture in them and adding water can make them slimy when cooked. Lay the mushrooms out on a dry kitchen towel for about 30 minutes before chopping. I chop most of the mushrooms into bite-size pieces and leave just a few as larger pieces.

In a large nonstick pan over medium-high heat, add 2 tablespoons of the butter and a drizzle of oil and heat until the butter is melted. (Adding the oil keeps the butter from browning.) Add the mushrooms and quickly sear, then remove them from the pan and place them in a medium bowl.

Add the remaining 2 tablespoons of the butter to the pan and heat until melted, then add the shallots and sauté until tender. Remove the shallots from the pan and add them to the bowl with the mushrooms, then set aside.

In a small bowl, beat the eggs, then add a small stream of cold water, no more than half a tablespoon. This lightens the eggs and will result in a fluffier omelet.

Return the pan to the stovetop over medium-high heat and pour in the eggs. Tilt the pan to disperse the eggs, then pull the center of the eggs to the edges of the pan. Tilt the pan to fill the voids. Do this about four times and then continue to cook the eggs for 4 minutes, so that the bottom begins to become golden-brown.

Add the mushroom mixture to one-half of the omelet and then fold over the other half, forming a half circle. Remove the pan from the heat.

Slide the omelet onto a plate and cut in half to serve. Season with salt and black pepper and sprinkle with the parsley.

Creamy Artichoke Heart Soup

During the early months of autumn, there is a period of time when we allow the plants in the kitchen garden to flower to the point of producing seeds. I always look forward to seeing our artichoke plants go into full flower and revel at the spiky and robust beauty of their vibrant purple heads. By the end of the summer, the last artichokes have been collected, and in abundant years, the hearts have been steamed and prepared for freezing. This soup is a lovely way to celebrate the best part of the artichokes and to enjoy a creamy mild soup that exemplifies their subtle flavor. You can easily use store-bought artichoke hearts, but just be sure to get the non-marinated type. Frozen artichoke bottoms or pieces can usually be found precooked, just thaw before use.

SERVES 4

1 (14-ounce / 400 g) can artichoke bottoms, approximately 8, drained

1 (10-ounce / 280 g) can artichoke hearts in water, drained

2 tablespoons butter

2 shallots, finely diced

1 medium celery stalk, finely diced

1 medium potato, peeled, cooked and diced

1 cup / 240 ml vegetable or chicken stock

2 cups / 480 ml heavy cream

Salt

Olive oil

8 thin slices of baguette

¼ cup / 60 ml crème fraîche for topping

Set aside 2 of the artichoke bottoms. Chop the remaining artichoke bottoms along with the artichoke hearts into small pieces (they will eventually be puréed, so they don't have to be perfect). In a large saucepan over medium heat, melt the butter and add the artichoke pieces, shallots, and diced celery. Cook for 5 minutes, until they begin to lightly caramelize.

Add the potatoes to the pot and then add the stock. Continue to cook for 20 minutes. Add the cream and salt to taste. Remove the pot from the heat and blend with an immersion blender or food processor.

Prepare the garnish by slicing the reserved artichoke bottoms into 8 pieces of even thickness. In a small sauté pan over medium-high heat, add a drizzle of oil and sear the artichoke bottom pieces then set aside.

Preheat the broiler.

Drizzle the baguette slices with olive oil and cook under the broiler on a sheet pan until golden and crispy.

To serve, ladle the soup into shallow bowls and top with the artichoke slices, a spoon of crème fraîche, and a few toasted baguette pieces in each bowl.

Queue de Boeuf Mijotée — Tender Stewed Oxtail

The broth in this stew, which straddles the fence between being a soup or a stew, is decadently rich because the collagen in the bones builds both the flavor and consistency of the nutritious cooking stock. Oxtail becomes fork-tender and is worth the effort to acquire for this recipe, but if you are unable to find oxtail at your local butcher, beef shoulder can be substituted. Be sure to cut the shoulder into large pieces (larger than stew size) so they can sustain the long cooking time. For a 2- to 3-pound / 1 to 1.5 kg shoulder, I would cut it into six large pieces. Add a few marrow bones to get a similar result. This hearty dish can also be served as a stew on a bed of puréed potatoes or if enjoyed as a soup, accompanied by a loaf of rustic bread. You will want to soak up every drop!

SERVES 4 TO 6

4½ pounds / 2 kg oxtail sections

Salt and freshly ground black pepper

3 tablespoons / 45 ml olive oil

1 large onion, diced

2 celery stalks, finely diced

2 medium carrots, diced

3 garlic cloves, sliced into thin pieces

2 tablespoons tomato paste

¾ cup / 180 ml red wine

6 cups / 1.5 L beef stock

4 cloves, or ⅛ teaspoon ground cloves

2 tablespoons apple cider vinegar

Preheat the oven to 325°F / 160°C.

Dry the meat on both sides with a paper towel and rub with salt and pepper.

In a large cast-iron Dutch oven or heavy-bottomed pot over medium-high heat, add 2 tablespoons of the oil and heat. Add the meat and brown evenly on all sides, then remove from the pot and set aside.

To the same pot over medium heat, add the onion, celery, carrots, garlic, and the remaining tablespoon of olive oil. Sauté the vegetables, while scraping the bottom of the pot. Sweat the vegetables (sauté on medium-low heat and allow them to become tender but not browned) for 5 minutes before adding the tomato paste. Continue stirring for about 3 more minutes until the paste is cooked, then add the wine. Continue to cook for several minutes to reduce and then add the stock, cloves, and vinegar.

Add the meat back into the pot. Be sure that the meat is submerged, adding more stock as needed, then cover the pot and place it in the oven.

Reduce the oven temperature to 300°F / 150°C. Check the meat after 2 hours. If your sections are small, they might cook more quickly. The meat should fall away from the bone slightly. After the 3-hour mark, continue to check once per hour. It is

continues >

QUEUE DE BOEUF MIJOTÉE,
continued

also important to taste and verify the texture. If the meat seems tough, it means that it needs at least 2 more hours. Don't be confused by thinking the meat is overdone; it should fall off the bone and have a melt-in-your-mouth tenderness.

Once the meat is cooked to extreme tenderness, gently remove it from the cooking juices and set it aside. Also remove some of the vegetables and the whole cloves with a slotted spoon and set aside. Return the pot to the stove and heat over medium-high to boiling, then turn down the heat to low and reduce the stock by about one-third. This is a low, long simmer. The stock will be thickened and decadently rich. Plate the meat with the reserved vegetables and add a ladle of the thickened sauce just before serving.

If you are lucky enough to have leftovers, the stewed oxtail can be stored in the refrigerator for 3 to 5 days. It is not recommended for freezing.

Cheese Soufflé

Cheesy, creamy, and light but so satisfying . . . it goes without saying that a soufflé has a well-known reputation for being a fussy French dish with a high failure rate. Both rustic in its simplicity and yet somewhat elegant, every cook should give it a try and will surely be won over! If you break it down, the recipe is simply adding beaten eggs to a classic béchamel sauce, flavored with nutty Gruyère cheese. I like to make individual soufflés in ramekins, but you can also use a single 8-inch / 20 cm soufflé bowl. Cheese soufflés cooked in individual molds tend to rise better than those prepared in a large mold. We love having soufflés with a green salad for lunch or as an appetizer for a cozy dinner. *(Pictured on pages 192–193.)*

SERVES 4 TO 6

Butter, for greasing the ramekins

1 teaspoon Dijon mustard

4 large egg yolks

1 cup / 240 ml Béchamel Sauce (page 24)

5 large egg whites, cold

3 ounces / 85 g Gruyère or other semi-firm cheese, such as Fontina or Gouda, freshly grated

Butter the interior of the ramekins. Place the ramekins in the refrigerator to chill while you prepare the soufflé mixture.

Preheat the oven to 375°F / 190°C.

Whisk the mustard and egg yolks into the prepared béchamel sauce. Be sure that the béchamel sauce is at room temperature or cool before adding the yolks.

Using a stand mixer fitted with the whisk attachment, or an eggbeater, beat the egg whites until they hold a peak. They should stick firmly to the whisk without any hard edges or lumps.

Fold in one-third of the egg whites into the yolk mixture. At this stage, you are only mixing lightly, and the soufflé batter will be streaky. Add the cheese and then the second third of the egg whites, this time folding until uniformly combined and pale yellow. Gently fold in the final portion of egg whites.

Gently ladle the batter into the prepared ramekins. Fill to about ½ inch / 1.5 cm from the rim, as the batter will expand.

Place the ramekins on a sheet pan and place in the oven. Bake for about 30 minutes (or for 45 minutes if using a single bowl), until the soufflé is fully risen and golden.

Remove the pan from the oven and transfer the ramekins to plates to serve immediately. Inevitably, the soufflés will fall, but if they are served or presented right away, you can enjoy the momentary puffs of these delicious creamy soufflés.

Choucroute Garnie

Choucroute garnie is the French term for "dressed sauerkraut." Although this dish is believed to have originated in Germany, Alsace and other parts of France claim it as their own. It is particularly popular in Normandy and can be purchased as a complete, ready-to-eat meal at both the autumn markets and local *boucheries*, or butcher shops. The dish consists of preparing fermented cabbage or sauerkraut with sausages and other salted meats and charcuterie and is sometimes served with boiled or steamed potatoes. It's important to use a good-quality sauerkraut, so check the label for unnecessary ingredients like sugar or preservatives. Sauerkraut should be vinegary and only slightly salty and still retain a little crunch or firmness. Since the meats are all precooked, this is an easy autumn dish to throw together when you want something cozy without a lot of effort.

SERVES 6

½ cup / 110 g goose fat or butter

2 (8-ounce / 225 g) containers store-bought sauerkraut, drained

6 whole juniper berries

3 bay leaves

1 teaspoon freshly ground black pepper

3 cups / 720 ml vegetable stock

1½ cups / 360 ml Alsatian wine, such as Riesling or Pinot Gris

2 pounds / 900 g small thin-skinned potatoes

2 pounds / 900 g Polish kielbasa, cut into 2-inch / 5 cm pieces

2 pounds / 900 g smoked ham hock

6 *saucisse* (smoked sausage) or Polish hot dogs

Whole grain mustard, for serving

Cornichon pickles, for serving

In a large Dutch oven or heavy-bottomed pot over medium heat, melt the goose fat. Add the sauerkraut, juniper berries, bay leaves, and black pepper then cover with the stock and wine. Add the potatoes and cover. Simmer for 30 minutes.

Add the kielbasa and ham hock and continue to simmer for 30 more minutes. Add the *saucisse* and heat for the final 10 minutes.

To serve, remove the smoked meats from the pot and layer on one side of a large serving platter. Add the sauerkraut and potatoes to the other side of the platter. Serve with whole grain mustard and cornichon pickles.

Porc au Cidre

Cider-Braised Pork Cheeks

I will never forget the first time I had pork cheeks. A chef I was interviewing had invited me to his kitchen early in the morning to document his mise en place, his preparations for the day's service. Tucked back on a small burner on his massive stove was a bubbly pot of steamy broth and meat that sent a waft of glorious aroma all the way to the dining room. When I asked him what he was making, he told me it was *Joues de porc à la Normande*, or cider-braised pork cheeks, also called jowls. I instantly knew what I would be ordering at dinner that evening and possibly the next night. Now, making it at home, I love serving this with little steamed potatoes and whole roasted tomatoes on the vine as a luxe garnish.

SERVES 4

3 pounds / 1.5 kg pork cheeks

2 tablespoons all-purpose flour

Salt and freshly ground black pepper

2 tablespoons butter

2 tablespoons olive oil, plus more as needed

1 medium onion, finely chopped

2 garlic cloves

2 celery stalks, diced

2 medium carrots, diced

3 cups / 720 ml fermented cider

1 bay leaf

3 sprigs of fresh thyme, or ½ tablespoon dried

2 tablespoons honey

1 pound / 450 g small to medium potatoes, steamed or roasted, for serving

Chopped fresh thyme and parsley, for garnish

Prepare the pork cheeks by thoroughly drying them with a kitchen towel and dusting with the flour evenly on all sides. Season with salt and pepper.

In a large Dutch oven or heavy-bottomed pot over medium heat, add the butter and oil and heat until the butter is melted. Place each pork cheek into the pot with tongs, moving them around to ensure they don't stick, then sear fully on each side to form a golden crust.

Remove the pork cheeks from the pot and place on a plate before sautéing the diced vegetables in the same pot. You can add a drizzle more oil as needed. Then add the onion, garlic, celery, and carrots to the pot over medium-high heat and sauté for 5 minutes. Add the cider and stir to deglaze the pot. Place the meat back into the pot.

Add the bay leaf, thyme, and honey. Reduce the heat to low and simmer, covered, for 2 hours. After 2 hours, test the pork by prodding with a fork. The meat should be completely tender and fall apart easily.

When the pork cheeks have finished cooking, remove the meat and vegetables with a slotted spoon. At this time, you can also remove any herb stems and the bay leaf. Bring the cooking stock up to a boil and reduce for about 20 minutes to thicken.

Plate the pork and vegetables with the cooked potatoes and hot cooking juices. Garnish with thyme and parsley.

Pommes Boulangère

Gratin Potatoes Cooked in Stock

I love the history behind country dishes. *Pommes boulangère* literally means "baker's potatoes" and originated in France centuries ago, when people in countryside villages did not own ovens of their own. The villagers would prepare dishes of potatoes and give them to the local baker to place in his hot bread oven after the day's batches of bread were done. The dish would slowly cook while the ovens cooled down and would be retrieved after the villagers attended Sunday mass. This dish can be made as a vegetarian option with the use of vegetable stock; a Savoyard version can be made with the addition of grated cheese and bacon. While some versions also call for white wine, I love the simplicity of the sliced potatoes that cook slowly and absorb the flavorful stock. It's a perfect side dish to serve with a roasted chicken or Sunday roast.

**SERVES 4 TO 6 AS
A SIDE DISH**

1 tablespoon butter

3 medium onions, thinly sliced

6 pounds / 2.75 kg potatoes, cut into ¼-inch / 6 mm-thick rounds

Salt and freshly ground black pepper

1 teaspoon dried thyme

4½ cups / 1 L chicken stock

1 bay leaf

1 sprig of rosemary (optional)

Preheat the oven to 325°F / 160°C. Butter a 2-quart / 2 L casserole dish.

Place a single layer of onions on the bottom of the prepared dish and then a layer of potatoes. Sprinkle each layer with salt and pepper, followed by some of the thyme. Repeat until all the onions and potatoes are used. Cover with the stock and then tuck in the bay leaf and the rosemary (if using).

Place the dish in the oven and bake for 45 to 60 minutes, until the stock has been absorbed and the potatoes are tender. Remove the bay leaf and rosemary sprig before serving.

Chicken Pot Pies

This is a simplified version of the original classic pot pie. It uses less pastry but packs in more flavor. In France, it is more of a stew *en croûte*, or creamy chicken and vegetables hiding under a cover of crispy and buttery pastry. My addition of precooked red, wild, and long grain rice adds texture and creates an even heartier dish. You might think I forgot the green peas that almost every pot pie recipe calls for. This is an intentional omission in homage of my childhood, when the green peas would remain orphaned at the bottom of my bowl or would be sneakily passed to my sister, who loved them. Feel free to use a store-bought roasted chicken for convenience or any cooked chicken meat you might have on hand. Along with using precooked potatoes, that's a real time-saver!

MAKES 4 INDIVIDUAL CROCKS

¼ cup / 60 g salted butter, plus more for buttering the crocks

1 tablespoon olive oil

4 shallots, diced

3 celery stalks, diced

3 medium carrots, chopped into ½-inch / 1.5 cm pieces

1 cup / 125 g chopped button mushrooms

⅓ cup / 40 g all-purpose flour

2 cups / 250 g diced cooked potatoes

3 cups / 720 ml chicken stock

1 teaspoon salt

¼ teaspoon white pepper

1 teaspoon dried thyme

2 cups / 250 g cooked blend of red, wild, and long grain rice

¾ pound / 340 g cooked, chopped chicken meat (about 4 cups)

½ cup / 120 ml cream

1 (16-ounce / 450 g) package puff pastry

1 large egg yolk, beaten, for brushing the pastry

Preheat the oven to 425°F / 220°C. Butter four ovenproof crocks and set aside.

In a large sauté pan over medium-high heat, add 2 tablespoons of the butter and the oil and heat until the butter is melted. Add the shallots, celery, carrots, and mushrooms and cook for 10 minutes, or until the carrots are tender. Add the remaining 2 tablespoons butter to the pan and once melted, add the flour. Cook the vegetables and flour for about 5 minutes, or until the raw flour taste is cooked out. Add the potatoes, stock, and the salt, pepper, and thyme. Fold in the cooked rice and chicken and then the cream. Stir until well combined, remove the pan from the heat, and cool to room temperature.

Remove the pastry from the refrigerator and place on a large sheet of parchment paper. First trace, then cut the pastry into rounds that are 1½ inches / 4 cm larger than the rim of the crocks. Fill each crock with the pot pie filling and then cover with the pastry rounds. Lightly poke holes into the tops of the pastry and brush with the egg yolk.

Bake until the pastry top is golden, about 30 minutes, and serve immediately.

Poule au Pot

Slow-Simmered Whole Chicken with Autumn Vegetables

The phrase a chicken in every pot has been attributed to the French king, Henry IV, who promised that, even as the country was facing terrible famines and hardship as a result of a long-lasting war, every home would have "a chicken in the pot" every Sunday. Since then, French people have associated *poule au pot* with a humble comfort dish that is widely cooked as a Sunday meal. This rustic and very healthy dish consists of a whole chicken cooked with vegetables in a flavorful broth. Traditionally, the vegetables consisted of leeks, carrots, and turnips; however, you can also add small thin-skinned potatoes that are a lovely addition in the flavorful broth. The broth itself is a bonus, since there will be plenty left over to use for other meals in the coming week.

SERVES 4 TO 6

1 (4-pound / 1.75 kg) whole farm-raised chicken

Salt and freshly ground black pepper

2 tablespoons duck fat or olive oil

1 cup / 100 g lardons or thick-cut smoked bacon, diced

1 large leek, cut into 3-inch / 7.5 cm pieces

3 carrots, chopped into 2-inch / 5 cm pieces

2 celery stalks, cut into 1-inch / 2.5 cm pieces

6 medium turnips, quartered

1 pound / 450 g thin-skinned potatoes (optional)

1 medium green cabbage, chopped

1 cup / 240 ml dry white wine

6 cups / 1.5 L chicken stock

4 sage leaves

2 sprigs of tarragon, or ½ tablespoon dried

Dry the exterior of the chicken with a kitchen towel and season with salt and pepper.

In a large heavy-bottomed pot over medium-high heat, melt the duck fat. Add the chicken to the pot and brown evenly on all sides.

Add the lardons, leeks, and carrots, tucking the lardons and vegetables in so that the chicken rests on top. Turn the heat down and allow the vegetables to sweat for about 5 minutes. Add the celery, turnips, and potatoes to the pot with the chopped cabbage on the top and tucked around the sides, then pour in the wine and stock and add the sage, tarragon, and salt and pepper to taste.

Cover and simmer on medium heat for 45 minutes to just over an hour, depending on the size of the chicken. The chicken should almost fall off the bone.

Serve large pieces of deboned meat in a shallow soup bowl with all the veggies and lots of broth.

Cassolettes de Saint-Jacques — Scallop Gratin

If you escape to the Normandy seaside in the fall, you can take advantage of the peak season for scallops. Festivals are hosted locally, and restaurants feature a variety of dishes that highlight scallops, called coquilles Saint-Jacques for the pretty flat shells that hold them, along with other local seafood. This *cassolette*, which means "small casserole" in French, highlights the subtle taste of the scallops in a delicate cream sauce, flavored with shallots and tarragon.

SERVES 4

1 pound / 450 g medium fresh scallops

5½ tablespoons / 80 g salted butter

3 shallots, finely minced

3 tablespoons / 23 g all-purpose flour

½ cup / 120 ml white wine

2 cups / 480 ml whole milk

1 teaspoon Dijon mustard

½ teaspoon dried tarragon

Salt and freshly ground black pepper

½ pound / 225 g cooked shrimp, peeled and deveined (31/35 count)

¼ cup / 25 g plain or seasoned breadcrumbs

Chopped fresh parsley, for garnish

Preheat the oven to 375°F / 190°C. Lay the scallops on a paper towel to absorb any extra moisture.

In a medium saucepan over medium heat, melt 4 tablespoons / 55 g of the butter, then add the shallots. Cook until tender and then add the flour. Reduce the heat to low and cook for 2 minutes to cook off the raw flour taste. Increase the heat to medium-high and add the wine. Heat until the mixture comes to a low boil, then add the milk. Reduce the heat to low, add the mustard and tarragon and simmer for 15 minutes to thicken. Add salt and pepper to taste.

In a medium casserole dish or in four individual gratin dishes or ramekins, place a small amount of the sauce and add the scallops (about 4 scallops per person). Add more sauce to cover the scallops and then add the shrimp. Top with the remaining sauce and sprinkle with the breadcrumbs. Cook for 10 minutes.

Garnish with the parsley.

Gratin de Haricots Blancs — Oven-Baked Beans

There are few things more satisfying than using canned and preserved provisions from the summer months for autumn and winter dishes. The secret to these flavorful beans comes from the delicious and rich Roasted Vegetable Sauce (page 107) that was made from the summer's harvest of tomatoes and vegetables. There is nothing that can compare to the creamy tender beans that cook slowly in the oven.

SERVES 4 TO 6

1 (1-pound / 450 g) package dried haricot blanc beans or other small white beans, such as navy or cannellini

8 cups / 2 L water, plus more for soaking

2 tablespoons butter

1 tablespoon olive oil

1 celery stalk, finely diced

1 medium carrot, chopped into ½-inch / 1.5 cm pieces

1 medium onion, diced

3 garlic cloves, thinly sliced

2 cups / 480 ml Roasted Vegetable Sauce (page 107) or plain tomato sauce with a vegetable bouillon cube added

Salt and freshly ground black pepper

1 tablespoon butter, melted (optional)

1 cup / 120 g breadcrumbs

8 strips thick-cut smoked bacon

Chopped fresh parsley, for garnish

Cover the beans in cold water and soak overnight.

Drain the beans and place them in a large pot with fresh water, covering them by 2 inches / 5 cm. Bring to a boil over high heat, then reduce the heat to low and simmer for 1 hour.

Drain the beans and put them into a large Dutch oven or a pottery bean pot.

Preheat the oven to 350°F / 180°C.

In the original pot over medium heat, add the butter and oil. Once the butter is melted, add the celery, carrots, onion, and garlic, and sauté for 5 minutes. Add the mixture to the Dutch oven along with the roasted vegetable sauce and 8 cups water. Add salt and pepper to taste.

Cover and place the pot in the oven and cook for 3 hours, until the beans are very soft and creamy. If more time is needed, check at 30-minute increments and add water or stock, if necessary, to prevent them from drying out. Cooking times can vary greatly based on the type of bean and how they have been stored.

Once cooked and completely soft, remove the pot from the oven. If you are using the beans later, put them into shallow glass dishes to cool evenly before covering and putting them in the refrigerator.

To finish the dish, preheat the oven to 375°F / 190°C.

In a small bowl, mix the melted butter with the breadcrumbs.

Add the beans to an ovenproof baking dish, sprinkle with the breadcrumbs, and lay the bacon strips across the top. Bake for 25 minutes or until the beans are heated through and the bacon is brown. Remove the dish from the oven and garnish with the parsley. Serve immediately.

Papi's Chicken with Calvados and Sautéed Apples

This recipe captures all the iconic flavors of Normandy and was one of my father-in-law's favorites. Made with farm-raised chicken, apples, mushrooms, and a delicious cream sauce of flamed Calvados, it blends elegance with the rusticity of country food. I suggest serving it with crispy potatoes that have been steamed and then finished to a golden crust by sautéing in duck fat. The name of the dish comes from the area of Pays d'Auge, which is an area in the heart of Normandy, and the *escalope* comes from the scallopini or thinly pounded breast of chicken.

SERVES 4

4 chicken breasts (each about 6 ounces / 170 g)

2 tablespoons butter

1 tablespoon olive oil, plus more as needed

8 ounces / 225 g mushrooms, champignons de Paris or button, sliced into ¼-inch / 6 mm pieces

2 medium shallots, finely chopped

⅓ cup / 80 ml Calvados or brandy

2 Gala or Golden Delicious unpeeled apples, cut into wedges

1½ cups / 360 ml chicken stock

⅓ cup / 80 ml crème fraîche

Salt and freshly ground black pepper

Golden Crust Potatoes (page 211), for serving

Wrap each chicken breast in two layers of parchment paper and pound with a rolling pin until about ½ inch / 1.3 cm thick.

In a large frying pan over medium heat, add the butter and 1 tablespoon of the oil and heat until the butter is melted. Add the chicken pieces and cook until golden, 3 to 4 minutes on each side. Remove the chicken from the pan and set aside.

Add another drizzle of olive oil to the same pan as needed, then add the mushrooms and sear just until becoming golden. Place the mushrooms on a plate and set aside.

Add the shallots to the pan with the apple slices. Sauté for about 5 minutes until both are tender.

Remove the pan from the burner and turn off all the burners before pouring in the Calvados, since alcohol is highly flammable. Once the pan is away from the stove, pour in the Calvados.

Return the pan to the heat and carefully light the pan with a torch or a lighter; be sure to step back from the stove while the Calvados ignites. When the flame is gone, increase the heat to medium-high, add the stock, and bring to a boil. Cook the sauce for about 10 minutes to reduce, then add the crème fraîche. Add the chicken back into the pan, followed by the mushrooms.

To serve, place one piece of chicken on each plate, top with the cream sauce and mushrooms, and arrange the apple slices around the edges. Salt and pepper to taste. Serve with the golden crust potatoes.

Golden Crust Potatoes

Once the cooler weather really hits in Normandy, I most often make creamy potato and root vegetable purées as side dishes for meats and stews. On occasion, I prefer options that have a contrasting texture but are still perfect to mop up some of the delicious sauce that accompanies most of our autumn dishes. Potatoes are by far the most versatile root vegetable for this purpose, and you will love the golden, crispy crunch of these lovely potatoes that are easily made in a two-step process. The duck fat, of course, lends a gourmet richness and makes all the difference in flavor and texture, but you can replace it with olive oil if you don't have duck fat on hand.

SERVES 4

Water, for steaming

1 pound / 450 g unpeeled small fingerling or thin-skinned potatoes

1 tablespoon butter

2 tablespoons duck fat or olive oil

1 garlic clove, halved

Fleur de sel, for finishing

In a steamer pot or a large stockpot fitted with a steamer basket, over high heat, add about 3 inches / 7.5 cm water. Place the potatoes in the basket; be sure the basket does not touch the water. Cover the pot, then cook for 15 minutes or until the potatoes are tender when poked with the sharp tip of a knife. Once steamed, lay the potatoes on a tea towel to cool to the point that you can handle them.

Once the potatoes are cool, cut the potatoes lengthwise in half with a sharp knife.

In a large sauté pan over medium-high heat, add the butter and duck fat. Once the butter and duck fat are hot and bubbly, carefully add the potatoes. You will want to be able to lay all the potatoes face down, skin side up in a single layer.

Leave the potatoes to brown and crisp on the first side for 5 minutes, testing occasionally by peeking at the surface of the potato to check for even cooking. Add the garlic, then flip the potatoes over and cook the skin side for 5 minutes. Toss the potatoes with the warmed garlic and oil right before transferring to a serving plate.

Serve immediately and finish with a sprinkle of fleur de sel.

the pear tree

In the winter of 2013, when we first saw what would become our home at Rabbit Hill, we walked the property, exploring it from end to end. Our minds were filled with wonder, thinking about the history of what we believed must have been a beloved farm at one time. Old buildings gave evidence that the farm once had vast orchards. There was a cider mill housed in a rotting thatch-roofed barn, its huge press still recognizable even though the floors and ceilings had caved in decades before.

All the trees were long gone, except for one, and the fields around the house were now occupied by tenant cows that used the fifteen or so acres for seasonal grazing. The solitary survivor of the many changes that the farm had seen was a large gnarly, thick-trunked beauty. This tree, which we assumed was an ancient apple tree, stood between the house and the cider barn and was the centerpiece of the view from my kitchen window.

That first spring, we watched with amazement as this huge tree filled with beautiful pastel blooms. Leaves were slow to follow and slightly more sparse, but I commended that tree for showing off in the best way she could to welcome us to our new home. A few months later, the first group of cows arrived. Since we

never saw the tractor or farmer that dropped them off, it was as if they had fallen from the sky. Suddenly, there were twenty-six cows gathered around the base of the tree.

Each morning, I would stand with my coffee in hand and look out at that tree, say *bonjour* to the cows, and gather my thoughts for the day. I would make crêpes for my daughter, who was then two years old, and it was our morning routine to share breakfast, while looking out and observing the herd of cows whom we had begun to designate as the ladies of Rabbit Hill.

As autumn approached, small green fruit started to develop on the scraggly branches of the tree, and I noticed that as soon as a fruit fell, there was an eager cow standing ready to swallow it up in one chomp. I could see that if I was going to find out what was growing on that tree, I would need to move fast. So, one afternoon, as the cows were in the lower part of the field, I put on boots, grabbed a bucket, and headed out to the tree. I gathered up the few dozen pale green fruits that were lying on the ground and suddenly realized that what I had thought was an apple tree was actually a pear tree! Most likely, they were cider pears, small and sour, but they were little beauties. Even

though there would be no pie or compote made from them, they were well worth saving from the hungry cows.

Every season after, I loved observing the change of the seasons through the silhouette of the grand old pear tree. The cows used the tree for their meet-up spot for gossip in the late afternoon and on other occasions our geese would stroll by and examine her massive roots with curiosity. If not for the cows, we thought it would be amazing to hang a tire swing, but at the same time did not want to stress the tree's old, perhaps brittle branches.

In the spring, the tree would be covered with blooms, although there were fewer and fewer each year. In the summer, the tree provided a small patch of shade during unexpected July heat waves. In the fall, her leaves would thin or be taken away in a sudden autumn storm, and in the winter, she would stand in the stark landscape with the snowy cider barn in the background.

From the first time I saw the pear tree I was mesmerized by her solitary stature of strength. The view from my kitchen window of that tree grounded me and provided calm in ways that are hard to describe. I would stand in my kitchen and look out at that tree when I had no words, was waiting for an answer or trying to find something to say. It was there when I needed to pay tribute, to celebrate, to say goodbye, to note sunrises and sunsets, full

moons, and rainbows. My daughter would crouch at its base to examine a bug or a leaf or chase a cat up its massive trunk.

Four years later, in December, at the end of one of the most challenging years for us as a couple and family, the tree fell, uprooted from the muddy soil as her massive roots gave way. I would never have believed that the simple loss of a tree could bring such sadness. It was as if that horrible and hard year was determined to deliver one final devastating blow before it exited.

In spring, after the final storm subsided, we took the parts of the tree away. One large piece of the trunk became a bench that sits in our potager, and others became pearwood bread boards that I use in my kitchen. I'm thankful to have had that tree, standing just beyond the kitchen window to remind me to pause, to notice, and to share . . . It stood as a symbol of resilience to the end.

I will never know why that one pear tree was the sole survivor of many centuries, weathering the countless storms and wind up until that day. I am a believer that it is the simple things that bring the most meaning to a life, and that sometimes things need to fall apart to grow into something new and that struggles can bring the most necessary growth. I believe deeply that somehow that tree knew that its last job was not to produce abundant fruit but to welcome a family, provide calm, and encourage new roots.

Gâteau au Chocolat

A decadent dark chocolate cake, this dessert is often the one that I choose for my birthday celebration each year. I never grow tired of its bitter sweetness and simplicity. The batter can be prepared in advance and baked about thirty minutes before you are ready to serve it. Be warned, it will be hard to resist once the sweet chocolate aroma fills your kitchen. Serve it warm with your favorite ice cream.

MAKES ONE 8-INCH / 20 CM ROUND CAKE

½ cup / 110 g salted butter, plus more for buttering the baking pan

4 ounces / 115 g fine-quality dark chocolate (at least 72% cacao)

¾ cup / 150 g sugar

3 large eggs

½ cup / 40 g unsweetened cocoa powder, plus more for sprinkling

Vanilla ice cream or Crème Anglaise (page 286), for serving

Preheat the oven to 350°F / 180°C. Butter an 8-inch / 20 cm round baking pan.

Chop the chocolate into small pieces and cut the butter into large cubes.

Add the chocolate and butter to the top of a double boiler or to a metal bowl, set over a saucepan of barely simmering water. Melt the chocolate with the butter, stirring until smooth.

Remove the pan from the heat and whisk the sugar into the chocolate mixture. Let it stand for 5 minutes to cool and then add the eggs and whisk well.

Sift the cocoa powder over the chocolate mixture and whisk until just combined. Pour the batter into the prepared cake pan and bake in the middle of the oven for 25 minutes, or until the top has formed a thin crust.

Remove the pan from the oven and place on a wire rack. Cool the cake for 5 to 10 minutes and then invert it onto a serving plate and dust with additional cocoa powder. Serve with vanilla ice cream or crème anglaise.

Far Breton

Far Breton is a custardy flanlike dessert that hails from Normandy's sister region on the west. With its rugged coastline and windy and temperamental climate, there is no question why one might crave this cozy, slightly boozy, and delicately sweet dessert. Not only did my mother-in-law grow up on a farm in northern Brittany, it is also the ancestral home on my father-in-law's side. This recipe is a nostalgic favorite.

SERVES 4 TO 6

⅓ cup / 80 ml dark rum, cognac, or brandy

8 ounces / 225 g pitted dried plums or prunes

3 large eggs, plus 1 large egg yolk

2 cups / 480 ml whole milk

½ cup / 100 g sugar

¼ cup / 60 g salted butter, melted and brought to room temperature, plus more for greasing the pan

½ teaspoon vanilla extract

⅔ cup / 80 g all-purpose flour, plus more for dusting the pan

One day ahead, in a medium heavy-bottomed saucepan over low heat, warm the cognac and add the dried plums. The plums will absorb all the liquid and become soft and sweet. Remove the pan from the stove, cover, and set aside.

Heat the oven to 400°F / 200°C.

In a large bowl or in the bowl of a large blender, mix the eggs and additional yolk with the milk and whisk or blend until combined. Add the sugar, melted butter, vanilla, and flour and whisk or blend until smooth. Cover the bowl and place in the refrigerator to chill for 2 hours.

Butter a 12 by 8 by 2-inch / 30 by 20 by 5 cm rectangular baking dish and dust with flour.

Lay the plums uniformly across the bottom, then cover with the custard batter. Bake for 45 to 50 minutes until golden on the top.

Serve warm or cold, cut into rectangular pieces.

Tarte Bourdaloue

Pear Tart with Almond Pastry Cream

Named for a famous patisserie in Paris, this tart traditionally features poached pears cooked in a *pâte sablée* pastry, on a bed of almond cream. My rustic version uses fresh, fully ripe pears with their skins on. A little splash of dark rum adds both a lovely enhancement to the red Anjou pears and also a perfect balance to the toasty flavor of the ground almonds in the filling. It's also fine to leave it out and substitute just a touch of almond extract. This tart can be served warm or chilled.

SERVES 6

1 recipe *pâte sablée* pastry (page 19)

7 tablespoons / 100 g unsalted butter, at room temperature

2 eggs

⅓ cup / 40 g sugar

¾ cup / 100 g almond flour

3 tablespoons rum (optional)

1 teaspoon vanilla extract

4 medium skin on, ripe Anjou pears sliced into eighths

Whipped cream for serving

Preheat the oven to 350°F / 180°C.

On a lightly floured surface, roll the pastry into a 10-inch / 25 cm diameter round, about ⅛ inch / 3 mm thick. Fit the pastry round into an 8 inch / 20 cm diameter tart pan. Roll the excess pastry around the rim and crimp the edges. Put the pastry in the tart pan into the refrigerator to chill while you prepare the almond filling.

Using a mixer, combine the softened butter, eggs, sugar, and flour and mix until creamy. Add the rum, if using, and the vanilla. Take the pastry from the fridge and spread the almond filling evenly across the pastry with a spatula. Press the sliced pears into the almond cream.

Bake for 30 minutes until the top is golden. Serve with whipped cream.

Apple-Quince Crumble

Quince is a fruit that looks as if it belongs in a moody still life photo. It looks something like a robust and irregular cross between an apple and a pear, and it has an odd fuzzy skin. When ripe, it is golden yellow and has an extremely hard flesh. You will need your sharpest knife and a good cutting board to cut it. This recipe features both quince and apples and has deep caramelized flavors and the homey crunch of a nutty crumble topping. Serve warm, in deep bowls with lots of ice cream or whipped cream.

SERVES 6 TO 8

6 quince, cut into ½-inch / 1.5 cm wedges

½ cup / 120 ml water

¾ cup / 150 g sugar

4 apples, cut into 2-inch / 5 cm chunks

2 tablespoons/ 30 g salted butter

¼ teaspoon ground cinnamon

FOR THE TOPPING

¼ cup / 55 g granulated sugar

¼ cup / 50 g dark brown sugar

½ cup / 70 g light whole wheat flour

¾ cups / 70 g rolled oats

¼ cup / 55 g cold butter, cut into small cubes

1 cup / 120 g coarsely chopped walnuts

Vanilla ice cream or lightly whipped cream, for serving

Because the quince will take more than double the cooking time of the apples, begin by first adding the quince to a large pot with the water and sugar and simmer on low heat for 1 hour. The quince will change in color from a pale yellow to a pretty rosy pink.

Once the quince are tender, add the apples, butter, and cinnamon. Cook on low heat for 10 minutes or until the apples are just starting to become soft but are still holding their shape.

Preheat the oven to 350°F / 180°C.

To make the topping, in a large bowl, combine the granulated and brown sugars, flour, and oats. Add the butter and mix with a fork or cut with two knives, until the butter is blended into course chunks. Add the walnuts and mix.

Spoon the quince and apple mixture into a 2-quart or (8 by 12-inch / 20 by 30 cm) casserole dish, spreading evenly, then add the crumble topping.

Bake in the oven for 30 minutes, or until the topping is crisp and browned and the fruit is bubbly. Cool slightly before serving with ice cream or whipped cream.

WINTER
L' HIVER

LONG, WET WINTER MONTHS in Normandy call for cozy gatherings with friends. Most older homes here have multiple fireplaces that are lit in the late afternoon to combat the shorter days and sudden drop in temperatures. With or without a fire in the fireplace, candles are a requisite, and I often line my kitchen counters with antique brass candlesticks, while I prepare to cook.

Typically, everyone stands around in the kitchen, and I long ago abandoned the idea of encouraging guests to take a comfortable seat in the living room while I finish dinner preparations. I have found that if not already in the kitchen, guests always migrate back into the warmth and good smells of my favorite space in the house. For that reason, we make sure their hands are filled with a drink and a small bite to open their appetites (and to prevent them from sampling the mise en place ingredients in little bowls on my counter!).

winter dishes featuring the warm flavors of provence

The winter season in Normandy is predictably wet. We often say, "Imagine if all of this rain were snow!" Perhaps that is why in my kitchen in the winter and early months of the new year, I lean toward the warm, rich flavors of southern France. I adore the plump garlic, multiple varieties of onions, salty brined olives, and sweet herbal honey that make their way into my winter menus at Rabbit Hill, and the rich tomato-based sauces that become even more vibrant as they stew for hours. After a winter walk on the beach or a chilly trip to our local market, there is nothing like returning home to a warm kitchen, building a fire, and watching winter Normandy storms from the comfort of a cozy chair or comfortable dining room.

During the cooler seasons, the traditional dishes that I cook are not only inspired by ingredients such as fennel, garlic, eggplant, potatoes, kale, and shallots that can be found in the village markets but also by what can be supplemented from shops and grocery stores.

Fennel is a flowering plant that is used both as an herb and as a vegetable. Native to Southern Europe along the Mediterranean, the plant has a subtle and sweet licorice flavor. The bulb can be cooked or eaten raw, the fronds can be used as a garnish or added to soups or sauces, and the seeds are commonly dried, used whole, or ground as an aromatic spice. Choose large bulbs that are white to pale green with fresh deep green stalks and fronds intact. Fennel bulbs will last for a few days on the counter and up to a week in the refrigerator.

Garlic is grown throughout France, which boasts over twenty thousand tons of garlic production each year. Called *ail* in French, the beautifully hued purple garlic *l'ail violet de Cadours*, found in the south, is my personal favorite for cooking during the winter months. It first appears in the markets in early summer (it can be planted as late as December in Provence) and once dried and cured can last about six months. When selecting garlic, look for large garlic bulbs that are firm with tight paper and are well dried. It helps to squeeze the bulb in your hand to make sure it is fresh and not rotten or dried beyond use. Garlic should be stored in a dry, dark place, in a drawer meant for onion and garlic storage or a pottery crock and will last several weeks if it is fresh when purchased. Garlic can be frozen once peeled and can be stored in an airtight container in the freezer for up to six months.

Eggplant, or aubergine in French, is grown from spring to late autumn and can be found year-round. It is rich in fiber and antioxidants. There are numerous varieties, but the most common is the dark purple to purplish-black oval or long variety. The skin should be shiny and firm with minimal blemishes. While many remove the skin, it contains a high level of vitamins and nutritional value. Eggplant lasts just a few days on the counter or up to five days if refrigerated.

The French prefer small thin-skinned potatoes, called *pommes de terre*, to larger thicker-skinned rustic potato varieties found elsewhere. Most commonly, they use a medium to small type called Charlotte, which has a pale, thin skin and can be long or oval. Similar to a Yukon Gold in the US, with their sweet and smooth flesh, Charlottes are perfect for steaming or boiling, roasting, and slicing for gratins. When choosing potatoes, select ones that have pale beige skin without any green or sprouting eyes and with only minor marks and spots. Although small blemishes and eyes can be removed and green areas peeled off, do not eat

tubers that have green below the skin level, since this can be mildly toxic if eaten in large quantities. Store potatoes in cool, dry, and dark containers or in pantry areas.

Kale, or *chou kale* in French, is considered an ancient crop or plant in France. Although kale peaked in popularity as a super food in the United States decades ago, it is referred to as a forgotten vegetable in France. Although it has many names and classifications, it is rarely seen in the markets and almost never in modern grocery stores. Eaten during hardship when food was scarce, much like cabbage, potatoes, and turnips, it disappeared after war times and it was only until the last ten years or so when it was reintroduced to farmers and eventually to other producers and the culinary world. Three types can be found in France: *kale frisée* (curly leaf kale); *kale de Russie* (red Russian kale), which is often called Italian kale; and *kale noire* (black kale), which is also known as cavolo nero. When selecting kale, look for kale that is firm and not wilted and deep green rather than yellowed. Kale stores well in the refrigerator and can be easily frozen after blanching for a few minutes in salted boiling water.

The French have long favored shallots for cooking. Milder and sweeter than a standard onion, they are more long than round and have a golden to pinkish-orange outer skin layer. I love the pink shallot, sometimes called the Jersey, which is small and has a rose or pale purple interior and tastes much like a red onion. For recipes that require a raw onion, I prefer shallots. They are often called for in salads and traditional vinaigrettes and are perfect for sauces. They are also lovely pickled or made into onion "jam," or confit. Shallots are always found in the markets and have a long shelf life when properly stored in a dark, dry, and cool location. When shopping for shallots, look for bulbs that are firm with dry paper and layers.

Rustic Warm Olives

Flavorful, warm, and tender olives, served with slices of fresh crusty baguette, are the perfect palette opener. For this appetizer, use the highest-quality olives you can find. Heating olives brings out their rich, oily flavor.

SERVES 4 AS AN APPETIZER

½ cup / 120 ml olive oil

1 garlic clove, minced

2 teaspoons fennel seeds

2 teaspoons dried oregano

2 tablespoons lemon juice

Zest of 1 lemon

Hot or sweet red pepper flakes for sprinkling (optional)

1½ cups / 270 g mixed olives, rinsed and drained

Baguette slices, for serving

In a small sauté pan over low heat, add the oil and gently warm. It's important not to heat the oil too quickly or allow it to brown. Add the garlic, fennel seeds, and oregano and stir for 1 minute. Then add the lemon juice and stir for 30 more seconds.

Remove the pan from the heat and add the lemon zest. Sprinkle in a desired amount of pepper flakes (if using).

Place the olives in a glass bowl and pour the oil mixture over the olives and cover. At this stage, the olives can be left overnight if you are preparing them in advance.

When ready to serve, transfer the olive mixture to an oven-safe crock or dish and place it in a 325°F / 160°C oven for 10 to 15 minutes or until warmed through. Serve along with slices of fresh baguette.

Crispy Sage Nuts

This is an addictive, salty, and flavorful mix of nuts, crispy herbs, and garlic—perfect for cocktail hour! I love serving these nuts and golden chips of garlic, along with Rustic Warm Olives (page 235) and bite-size pieces of rustic bread.

MAKES 4 CUPS / 575 G

¼ cup / 60 ml olive oil

4 to 8 large garlic cloves, cut into ⅛-inch / 3 mm slices

12 sage leaves

3 sprigs of rosemary, stems removed, leaves finely chopped

4 cups / 530 g mixed pecans and almonds, roasted and lightly salted

Rustic crusty bread, torn into bite-size pieces

In a small sauté pan over low heat, warm the oil, then add the garlic. The garlic pieces should be large enough to crisp evenly as they cook. Slowly brown the garlic until golden, being careful not to burn it. You may have to remove the pan from the heat multiple times.

Cut the sage using a chiffonade technique, which is done by stacking several leaves on top of one another followed by rolling the whole leaves into small tubes and then cutting into thin strips. Add the sage strips to the warming oil along with the rosemary. Once the herbs are crispy, pour the mixture over the nuts and toss until covered with the herbs and oil.

Serve warm or store in an airtight container in the refrigerator for up to 2 days.

Creamy Winter Garlic Soup

This soup is a mild and rich purée of a slowly cooked confit of garlic that is sure to warm and satisfy. I first made this soup for a group of friends in Los Angeles, California, to celebrate our engagement. I have been making it almost every winter since! At the time, I remember doubting the amount of garlic the recipe called for, for fear that it would be too sharp and overwhelm the soup, but the soup is actually lovely and mellow in flavor.

SERVES 4 TO 6

2 tablespoons olive oil

4 to 6 heads of garlic (about 16 cloves), thinly sliced

4 medium shallots, finely diced

2 tablespoons salted butter

½ teaspoon salt

½ teaspoon freshly ground black pepper

8 cups / 2 L chicken or vegetable stock

1 baguette, torn into bite-size pieces

⅓ cup / 80 ml crème fraîche

Croutons or buttered, toasted baguette, for serving

In a Dutch oven or heavy-bottomed soup pot over low heat, warm the oil. Add the garlic and shallots. (Although it might be time-consuming to cut the garlic into thin slices rather than crushing it, this allows it to become golden-brown because it cooks more slowly and more uniformly.) Gently sauté the garlic and shallots and then add the butter. Be very careful not to allow the garlic to get too brown. Increase the heat to medium-low and cook the garlic and shallots slowly until completely tender, about 30 minutes. You should be able to mash the garlic easily with a spoon to test for doneness. Add the salt and pepper to taste.

Add the chicken stock and stir. Let simmer for about 15 minutes before adding the torn pieces of baguette. The smaller the pieces, the faster they will dissolve in the soup. Once the baguette pieces are completely softened, remove the pot from the stove and using a regular or immersion blender, purée the soup until silky.

Return the pot to low heat and stir in the crème fraîche. At this stage you can test for saltiness. If your stock has a decent amount of salt, you will not want to add more.

Serve with croutons. The soup can be stored in a covered container in the refrigerator for up to 3 days.

Braised Fennel and Artichoke Hearts

Fennel, a prized culinary herb native to Southern Europe and the Mediterranean, has a distinct licorice or anise flavor when eaten raw, and a savory and slightly sweet, mild flavor when cooked. This dish will surprise those friends and family who think they don't like fennel—they will be asking for more! This dish is also versatile when served as an appetizer on *tartine,* small pieces of toast, tossed with pasta, or even added to pizza or flat bread.

SERVES 4

2 tablespoons salted butter

1 tablespoon olive oil

2 large fennel bulbs, sliced into ¼-inch / 6 mm pieces, plus fronds for garnish

1 (14-ounce/ 400 g) jar artichoke hearts

6 cloves Garlic Confit (page 256)

2 tablespoons garlic oil from the reserved oil of the Garlic Confit

Buttered, toasted baguettes, for serving

Pinch of fleur de sel, for finishing

Preheat the oven to 375°F / 190°C.

In an ovenproof sauté pan over low heat, add the butter and oil and heat until butter is melted. Add the fennel pieces. Increase the heat to medium and slowly sauté until the fennel becomes tender.

Drain the artichoke hearts. I always test one to gauge the saltiness. Add the artichoke hearts to the pan and gently turn the vegetables to ensure they are starting to become golden but not so much that they fall apart or lose their shape.

Slightly mash the garlic confit cloves and add them to the pan with the garlic oil. Arrange the fennel and artichokes in a single layer and place the pan in the oven. Bake for 25 minutes. Turn the layer of vegetables once so that both sides will be browned and then place the pan under the broiler for 5 minutes. Remove the pan from the oven and set aside to cool for 5 minutes.

When you are ready to serve, arrange the vegetables on a platter and garnish with the fennel fronds.

Serve the vegetables on toasted baguettes, using the oil from the pan to finish each toast. Add a pinch of fleur de sel for the perfect last touch!

Tomato-Fennel Bisque

I make this one-pot, oven-to-stove-to-table, hearty tomato soup during the winter months, when I am seeking a simple soup that is packed with unexpected flavors. Guests will be intrigued with the sweet and subtle flavor of the braised fennel and tomatoes that are slowly roasted prior to becoming the base for this delicious soup! Roma tomatoes work well in this recipe because of their lower juice content and thick flesh that cooks slowly. Romas can also be found in stores during the winter months and are ideal for cooking.

SERVES 4 TO 6

3 tablespoons / 45 g salted butter

1 tablespoon olive oil

1 large fennel bulb, finely diced

2 shallots, finely diced (about 3 tablespoons)

4 to 6 Roma tomatoes, quartered

¼ cup / 60 ml dry white wine

3 cloves Garlic Confit (page 256)

1 bay leaf

3 (14.5-ounce / 411 g) cans diced tomatoes

4 cups / 960 ml vegetable stock

½ cup / 120 ml heavy cream

Chiffonade of fresh basil, or ½ tablespoon dried basil, for finishing (optional)

Crème fraîche, for finishing

Preheat the oven to 425°F / 220°C.

In a large Dutch oven over medium heat, warm the butter and olive oil. Add the fennel, shallots, and Roma tomatoes. Once combined, move the pot to the oven, cover, and roast the fennel and tomato mixture for 30 minutes.

Remove the pot from the oven and place it back on the stovetop over medium heat. The fennel should be tender, and the tomatoes will have started to break down. Add the wine and scrape down the sides and bottom of the pot to deglaze. Add the garlic confit cloves, bay leaf, and diced tomatoes, then cover with the veggie stock. Turn down the heat to low and simmer for 1 hour.

The final step is to add the cream. Be sure the soup is not boiling before adding the cream. For a silky texture, I use an immersion blender as a final step, but if you prefer a more rustic texture, you can skip this step. Be sure to remove the bay leaf before blending and serving.

The soup can be topped with fresh basil and a spoonful of crème fraîche. I love serving this vibrant soup with warm Socca (page 244).

Socca

Socca is a flat pancake that originated in the south of France. While some consider it to be a type of flat bread, it's made from a batter rather than from a dough. A beloved snack and street food, it is created from a mixture of chickpea flour, water, and olive oil. Before baking, be sure to let the batter rest for at least one hour—two is even better, and set your oven to the highest temperature for the perfect combination of soft and crispy. Using a cast-iron pan is the best choice, since the cooking method mimics a bread oven and the heat is quite high. I love making socca right before guests arrive for an aperitif. The smell of the cumin and the toasty aroma as the pancake becomes golden will have everyone gathering around trying to grab the first one that comes out of the oven. For a crowd, use a large (9-inch / 23 cm) diameter round pan, and then cut the socca in triangles similar to pizza slices. For a cocktail gathering, serve socca with Rustic Warm Olives (page 235) and Crispy Sage Nuts (page 237).

MAKES 4 TO 6 SOCCAS

1 cup / 140 g chickpea flour

¾ teaspoon sea salt

½ teaspoon ground cumin

1 cup plus 2 tablespoons / 270 ml cold water

2½ tablespoons olive oil

Freshly ground black pepper, assorted chopped fresh herbs, or sautéed onions (optional)

Green salad, for serving (optional)

In a large bowl, mix the flour, salt, and cumin together. Add the cold water and whisk until thoroughly combined. Cover the bowl with parchment paper or a tea towel and allow to rest for 1 to 2 hours.

Preheat the oven to its maximum temperature, 475°F to 500°F / 250°C to 260°C. Heat an empty large cast-iron pan by placing it in the hot oven for 10 minutes.

Remove the pan from the oven and switch on the broiler. Add the oil to the hot pan just before pouring in the batter. Use only enough batter to cover the bottom of the pan in a thin layer. Place the pan in the oven about 4 inches / 10 cm below the broiler coils. Cook for about 7 minutes, until the socca is golden-brown with a few bubbles on top. Repeat with the remaining batter.

Remove the pan from the oven and top with pepper, fresh herbs, or sautéed onions, if you wish. Serve along with a green salad.

Roast Pork and Winter Root Vegetables

In France, there are specific types of pork that are designated in quality and identification not only by where the pigs are raised but also by their diet. I have found there is a vast difference in quality between industrial factory-raised pork and the meat from pigs that have been allowed to live more naturally and have access to a varied diet of foraged herbs, plants, and nuts. In fact, it leads me to believe that it is worth the extra effort to source "kindly raised" meats, even when the cost is greater. In this dish, the unusual method of searing a pork roast and then resting before slow cooking will guarantee the success of what is one of my favorite Sunday meals!

SERVES 4 TO 6

1 (3-pound / 1.5 kg) boneless pork roast

5 tablespoons / 75 ml olive oil, divided

Salt and freshly ground black pepper

2 large celery stalks, cut into 3-inch / 7.5 cm pieces

4 medium carrots, chopped into 3-inch / 7.5 cm diagonal slices

4 medium shallots, quartered

2 medium leeks, cut into 3-inch / 7.5 cm pieces

4 medium parsnips, halved or quartered

2 cups / 480 ml chicken or vegetable stock

1½ cups / 360 ml dry white wine

Salt-Roasted Potatoes (page 249), for serving

Preheat the oven to 500°F / 260°C.

Dry the roast on all sides with a kitchen towel and then rub with 1 tablespoon of the oil and the salt and pepper.

Heat a large cast-iron pan or gratin dish over high heat. Add 2 tablespoons of the oil and sear the roast on all sides. Once uniformly seared, place in the oven and roast for 15 minutes.

Remove the pan from the oven and allow the pork to rest on the stovetop for 30 minutes. In the meantime, turn down the oven to 325°F / 160°C.

Arrange the celery, carrots, shallots, leeks, and parsnips around the roast and drizzle with the remaining 2 tablespoons of oil before returning the roast to the oven. Wait for 10 minutes and then add 1 cup / 240 ml of the stock. Cover the pan and return the roast to the oven and cook for 1 hour.

Using a thermometer, test the temperature of the meat; it should be in the range of 140°F to 145°F / 60°C to 63°C. The roast will continue to cook after it is removed from the oven, so taking it out at just under ensures a perfect roast. Remove the roast from the pan and place it on a cutting board to rest. Remove the vegetables and put them on a serving plate or in a bowl.

Set the pan with any cooking juices on the stove over medium heat. Add the wine to the pan and deglaze, scraping down the browned bits. Bring to a full boil and reduce the wine slightly before adding the remaining 1 cup / 240 ml of the stock. Simmer for 5 more minutes. Reduce the heat under the pan to low to keep the sauce warm until ready to serve.

Slice the meat thinly and serve with the vegetables and potatoes. Spoon the sauce over the pork just before serving.

Salt-Roasted Potatoes

During the winter months, we often indulge in a quiet day of relaxation and fireplace cooking. Salt roasting is a cooking method often used in France, and it is one of the easiest cooking techniques, delivering moist and flavorful food! Grey sea salt, or *sel gris* as it's known in France, can be found at all grocery stores and food shops in France and in other parts of the world, at specialty markets and online. The higher moisture content of grey sea salt is a must to keep the potatoes "steaming" while roasting. In a pinch, you can use regular white coarse sea salt or kosher salt if grey salt is not available.

**SERVES 4 TO 6 AS
A SIDE DISH**

2 cups / 500 g grey sea salt

1½ pounds / 680 g small thin-skinned potatoes, such as Yukon Gold or fingerling

4 sprigs of fresh rosemary

3 sprigs of fresh thyme

6 garlic cloves, quartered

In a heavy cast-iron Dutch oven with a lid, add the salt until it covers the entire bottom of the pot, about 1½ inches / 4 cm deep. Wash and dry the potatoes, then arrange in a single layer on top of the salt. Top with the rosemary and thyme, gently pushing the stalks into the salt. Tuck the garlic cloves among the potatoes.

If using the fireplace method, cover the pot and place it directly on top of the hot coals or on a cooking rack. Cook for approximately 45 minutes to an hour or more, depending on the size of the potatoes and the heat of your fireplace. These potatoes can also be cooked in a lidded BBQ.

Fireplace cooking is not an exact science, and the overall cooking time might vary. If using an oven, preheat the oven to 425°F / 220°C.

Cover the pot and roast the potatoes for 30 to 40 minutes. Check for doneness by poking with a sharp knife. When cooked through, the skins will be dry and crispy, and the interior of the potatoes will be moist and creamy! Remove the potatoes from the pot and discard the salt before serving.

Confit d'Échalotes — Tangy Shallot Jam

I think you will find endless uses for this sweet and tangy confit of shallots. This is a staple in my pantry during the winter months, and it is lovely on savory tarts, works its way into sauces, and is always on the side of roasted meats. Because of its vinegar content, it can be stored for several months in a sealed jar in the refrigerator. Keep extra jam in tightly sealed jars to be ready to top appetizers of toasted baguettes and salty goat cheese.

MAKES 2 CUPS / 480 ML

2 pounds / 900 g medium shallots or small red onions

2 tablespoons olive oil

¾ cup / 150 g sugar

1½ cups / 360 ml balsamic vinegar

½ cup / 120 ml red wine vinegar

1 teaspoon salt

Peel the shallots and cut the larger ones in half.

In a medium sauté pan over low heat, warm the oil. Add the shallots and cook slowly until they become tender but not browned, about 20 minutes.

In a small bowl, combine the sugar, vinegars, and salt. Add to the pan with the shallots and simmer for 40 minutes. Remove the pan from the heat and set aside to cool.

Store the shallots in a sealed jar in the refrigerator. The flavor will intensify after storing for a few days.

Toulouse White Bean Soup

Soups made with hearty beans are quintessential comfort food during the wet and windy months in Normandy. Everyone in our family loves this creamy and filling soup. For the *saucisse fumé*, or smoked sausage, you can use any smoked sausage like kielbasa, and for the lardons, you can substitute thick-cut smoked bacon or pancetta. All great soups start with stunning bouillon stock or broth. I learned early on that prepared broths are not available in cans or boxes here in France as they are in the United States, so I soon became accustomed to making stock every time I cook a chicken or ham or have various bones on hand.

SERVES 4 TO 6

1 tablespoon olive oil

3 ounces / 85 g lardons

1 large onion, diced

2 carrots, diced

2 celery stalks, diced

2 garlic cloves, thinly sliced

1 leek, finely chopped

4 medium potatoes, chopped into 1½-inch / 4 cm pieces (about 3 cups / 450 grams)

6 cups / 1.5 L Savory Ham Stock (page 33) or Golden Chicken Broth (page 30)

1 (16-ounce / 454 g) can small white beans, such as navy or coco blancs, drained and rinsed

1 teaspoon dried thyme

1 cup / 150 g cubed or chopped *saucisse fumé*

Sliced green onion, for garnish

In a large Dutch oven or heavy-bottomed pot over medium heat, warm the oil, then add the lardons, onion, carrots, and celery and sauté for 5 minutes before adding the garlic and leek. Add the potatoes and then cover with stock. Turn down the heat to low and simmer until the potatoes are tender, about 15 minutes.

Add the beans and *saucisse fumé*. Simmer for another 30 minutes.

When ready to serve, garnish with sliced green onion.

Pork Meatballs with Kale and Beans

On especially blustery winter days, my body craves something filling and flavorful. Meatballs always remind me of the comfort of a meatloaf in bite-size portions, and I basically follow the same technique to make them. Although this recipe is noted as pork meatballs, it is actually a 2:1 ratio of pork and beef. The beef adds the extra fat that is needed, since pure pork meatballs can often be quite dry. You can use pre-ground meat, or if you grind your own, as we do in France, pork shoulder and stew beef have the perfect proportion of fat when combined at a 2:1 ratio.

SERVES 4 TO 6

2 pounds / 900 g ground pork

1 pound / 450 g ground beef

1½ tablespoons herbes de Provence

1 teaspoon pure garlic powder

¾ cup / 100 g breadcrumbs

2 egg yolks

Salt and white pepper

2 tablespoons olive oil

2 cups / 480 ml Summer Potager Tomato Sauce (page 106)

1 large bunch of curly leaf kale, chopped (about 2 cups / 140 g)

2 tablespoons butter

Splash of lemon juice

1 (16-ounce / 454 g) can white beans such as navy, great northern, or cannellini

1 (14-ounce / 411 g) can crushed tomatoes

1 teaspoon dried oregano

1 teaspoon dried thyme

1 teaspoon dried basil

Grated Parmesan cheese, for sprinkling

Begin by preparing the meatballs. In a large bowl, combine the ground pork and beef with the herbes de Provence, garlic powder, breadcrumbs, and egg yolks. Season with salt and pepper. Using your hands, form the meat mixture into large meatballs. I like to make 3 to 4 large meatballs per person.

In a large sauté pan over medium heat, warm 1 tablespoon of the oil, then add the meatballs and cook until evenly browned.

Preheat the oven to 375°F / 190°C.

Once the meatballs are browned, top them with the tomato sauce and place the pan in the oven to stay warm and to finish cooking through, about 20 minutes.

Wash and chop the kale, removing the large stems.

Set a second large sauté pan over medium heat and add the remaining tablespoon of oil and the butter. Once the butter has melted, add the kale and sauté for several minutes, or until tender. Add the lemon juice and salt to taste. Add the beans, tomatoes, oregano, thyme, and basil. Heat the mixture until it begins to bubble and is heated through, then remove the pan from the heat.

Serve the meatballs on top of the kale and beans and sprinkle with the Parmesan cheese.

Garlic Confit

Confit is a popular French cooking method, where food is submerged in fat or oil and slowly cooked at a low temperature. This recipe results in deliciously soft and perfectly cooked mild garlic that can be used as a spread or a paste in cooking or as a richly flavored oil to drizzle on bread, use in salad dressings, or for cooking other dishes. You can choose either a mild-tasting oil like grapeseed oil or a traditional olive oil.

MAKES APPROXIMATELY 2 CUPS / 480 ML

3 heads of garlic, cloves separated and peeled

1½ cups / 360 ml olive oil

Preheat the oven to 225°F / 110°C.

Place the cloves in a small cocotte or miniature Dutch oven and cover with the oil. Be sure that all the cloves are completely submerged. Cover and bake in the oven until the cloves are golden brown and tender, about 2 hours, depending on the size of the cloves. Remove the pot from the oven and bring to room temperature before storing.

Store the confit in an airtight container in the refrigerator. Be sure to use within 2 weeks.

Duck à la Provençale

I served this dish for the first time over twenty-five years ago, while we still lived in the United States. I made it for our first French Friends-giving, after I learned that our French friends were not keen on turkey. I can't count the times I have made it since, but it's probably in the hundreds, often as a celebration meal and always for a table full of people I love. The slow confit of the duck is presented in a zesty tomato and green olive sauce and is lovely served on a bed of creamy polenta. *(Pictured on page 260.)*

SERVES 4

DUCK

2 large onions, quartered

1 bunch of celery (about 6 to 8 stalks), cut in halves or thirds

1 large bunch of parsley

4 to 6 bay leaves

8 garlic cloves, halved

1 tablespoon dried thyme

1 (5 to 6-pound / 2.3 to 2.75 kg) duck

Olive oil

Salt and freshly ground black pepper

2 tablespoons herbes de Provence

½ cup / 120 ml dry white wine

1 cup / 240 ml vegetable or chicken stock

1 tablespoon tomato paste

1½ cups / 270 g French green olives

Preheat the oven to 475°F / 250°C.

To prepare the duck, chop the onions and celery into large pieces and place them in a large roasting pan. Layer with the entire bunch of parsley, both leaves and stems, ripped into pieces as needed to fit the pan (reserve a small amount of parsley to finely chop for garnish). Sprinkle the bay leaves, garlic, and thyme evenly over the herbs and vegetables.

Next, cut the duck in half by carefully cutting along one side of the backbone. I use poultry scissors and a cleaver since the duck bones are quite dense. Remove the wings and neck from the duck; these can be reserved for making stock. Prick the duck skin all over with a fork and rub the duck with olive oil, salt and pepper, and 1 tablespoon of the herbes de Provence.

Set the duck halves, cut sides down, on the bed of vegetables and roast for 25 minutes. Prick the duck skin again, cover the pan with aluminum foil, and reduce the oven temperature to 300°F / 150°C. Roast the duck for about 3 hours longer, until the meat is very tender and most of the fat has rendered. Once the duck has finished cooking, remove from the pan, set aside on a platter, and cover.

Strain the pan juices and fat from the vegetables. (I recommend using a fat-separating pitcher as you will need to pour off quite a bit of the rendered fat; filter this and save it for use at another time.) Pour just the juices into a saucepan.

Place the saucepan with the juices over low heat, add the wine and stock, and cook at a low simmer until the sauce is reduced by almost half. Add the tomato paste and the remaining 1 tablespoon of the herbes de Provence. Once the stock has thickened, add the olives.

POLENTA

4 cups / 960 ml water

Salt

1 cup / 140 g yellow polenta

3 tablespoons / 45 g salted butter, plus more as needed

¼ cup / 60 ml crème fraîche

Before finishing the duck, make the polenta. In a large pot over high heat, add the water and some salt, and bring to a boil. Add the dry polenta to the pan of boiling water and stir in the butter. Follow the specific instructions for cooking on the package as there are various types and grinds; some are packaged as instant, and others will be slower to cook. Continue to stir the polenta until it is thick but not solid. If the polenta rests and becomes too thick, you can thin it with a small amount of stock. I always add crème fraîche and a touch of butter to the polenta before plating the dish.

To finish the duck, preheat the broiler.

Place the roasted duck pieces on a large baking sheet. Broil for about 5 minutes, or until the duck is warmed through and the skin is crisp. Due to the fat, the duck can brown quickly, so be careful not to char the skin.

Serve the duck parts on the bone or remove the duck meat to serve on the polenta. I think that it presents best in large pieces without the bones, but I have done it both ways. Ladle the olive sauce on top of each serving and serve extra sauce on the side in a small pitcher.

Bouillabaisse

This traditional dish originates in Provence in the town of Marseilles. I think it would be safe to say that there are hundreds of varieties—some with just fish, many with shellfish, and I am even aware of one with chicken. The recipes range from very simple to quite complex, but remember, the original dish was rustic and delicious rather than a refined and elegant dish and was created as a way for fishermen to make a basic stew to use up their "undesirable" fish and seafood. The dish is usually served with rouille, a spicy mayonnaise that is spread on thick slices of country bread and floated on the bouillabaisse when served.

SERVES 6

2 to 3 tablespoons / 30 to 45 ml olive oil

3 shallots, finely diced

2 carrots, chopped into a small dice

½ fennel bulb, diced

1 yellow or red bell pepper, cut into ½-inch / 1.5 cm pieces

2 medium garlic cloves, crushed

3 (14.5-ounce / 411 gram) cans diced tomatoes, or 4 to 5 medium tomatoes, seeded and chopped

1 (3-inch / 7.5 cm) strip of orange peel

6 cups / 1.5 L Flavorful Fish Stock (page 31)

3 pounds / 1.5 kg mixed shellfish, such as mussels, clams, and shrimp

3 pounds / 1.5 kg firm white fish like cod or sea bass

1 baguette

Traditional Rouille (page 264) or store-bought, for serving

In a large pot over medium heat, warm the oil, then add the shallots, carrots, fennel, bell pepper, and garlic. Sauté for about 5 minutes. Add the tomatoes and orange peel and when the mixture starts to bubble, add the stock. Reduce the heat to a low simmer and cook for 30 minutes. Keep the broth at a low to medium simmer, since you want a slight reduction but not a rapidly boiling stock.

Add the shellfish to the pot. If you are using precooked prawns or shrimp, add them last just to warm. Once the shells have opened, add the fish and cook until the pieces of fish are cooked through and flaky.

Discard any unopened shellfish. Don't forget to remove the orange peel before serving; this is the mystery ingredient that, along with the fennel, makes the cooking broth so fragrant.

Serve with the baguette and rouille.

Rouille: Two Ways

Rouille can be found in gourmet shops in small jars or easily made at home. There are multiple recipes from the traditional to faster but equally tasty shortcut ones. I recommend using *piment d'espelette*, which is a flavorful and perfectly spicy pepper grown in the Basque region of France. You can substitute Aleppo pepper or a mixture of Spanish paprika and cayenne. If you have time to make rouille from scratch, you will love the first method. If you just want to enjoy the flavors without the added work of the traditional method, try the second one.

Traditional

MAKES ¾ CUP / 180 ML

1 red bell pepper, roasted and peeled

4 slices of baguette, cut 2½ inches / 6.5 cm thick and soaked in about ½ cup / 120 ml Flavorful Fish Stock (page 31)

½ teaspoon *piment d'espelette*

1 tablespoon lemon juice

1 large egg

1 small garlic clove

¼ cup / 10 g fresh parsley

1 teaspoon sea salt

⅓ cup / 80 ml extra-virgin olive oil

Using a food processor, purée the bell pepper, soaked baguette, *piment d'espelette,* lemon juice, egg, garlic, parsley, and salt until smooth. Slowly add the oil while processing to form a paste or mayonnaise-like texture.

Store in an airtight container in the refrigerator until ready to use. Traditional rouille should be used within 3 days.

Easy Homemade

MAKES 1 CUP / 240 ML

8 to 10 saffron threads

1 cup / 240 g mayonnaise

2 garlic cloves, minced

½ teaspoon *piment d'espelette*

½ teaspoon smoked paprika

Salt and freshly ground black pepper

In a small glass bowl, combine the saffron, mayonnaise, garlic, *piment d'espelette,* and paprika. Season with salt and pepper to taste and whisk until well blended. Make 1 day or at least several hours ahead of time for best flavor.

Store in an airtight container in the refrigerator until ready to use. Use within 3 weeks.

Bohémienne — Eggplant and Tomato Casserole

This is a richly flavored, slowly stewed dish that is frequently enjoyed in southeastern Provence. Delicious and versatile, it features a crunchy breadcrumb gratin topping and can be served in individual casserole dishes for cozy charm. The name bohémienne is the common name given to this dish, so named because artists and gypsies in the south of France made this dish during the 19th century.

SERVES 6

2 large eggplants

¼ cup / 60 ml olive oil

2 red onions, diced

2 garlic cloves, thinly sliced

4 thick-fleshed tomatoes, such as Roma, coarsely chopped

3 (15-ounce / 425 g) cans diced tomatoes in purée

2 bay leaves

2 teaspoons dried thyme

1 tablespoon herbes de Provence

¼ cup / 60 ml balsamic vinegar

2 tablespoons butter, melted

1 cup / 120 g seasoned breadcrumbs, or plain breadcrumbs mixed with 1 tablespoon herbes de Provence

4 to 6 anchovy fillets, finely diced

¼ cup / 8 g grated cheese, such as Parmesan or Asiago

Preheat the oven to 350°F / 180°C.

Cube the eggplant into small ½-inch / 1.5 cm squares with the skin on, unless the skin is very thick (this should yield about 4 cups / 325 g).

In a medium sauté pan over medium heat, add 2 tablespoons of the oil and warm. Add the onion and sauté for 2 to 3 minutes, then add the eggplant and the remaining 2 tablespoons of oil. Add the garlic, being careful not to overbrown it. Cook the eggplant until golden-brown, then add the chopped tomatoes, diced tomatoes with their liquid, bay leaves, thyme, and herbes de Provence. Reduce the heat to low and simmer the mixture for 5 minutes. Add the balsamic vinegar and stir to combine.

Remove the bay leaves. Transfer the mixture to a casserole or individual cocottes and bake, uncovered, for 20 minutes.

Remove the pan from the oven and top with the butter, breadcrumbs, and anchovies. Sprinkle with the cheese and return the pan to the oven to cook for 5 more minutes. Then toast or brown the breadcrumb topping under a broiler, as needed.

Red Wine Risotto

This is a simple dish that creates instant festivity, and the slow and forgiving technique is ideal for entertaining, when you have many things to attend to. Not only does this recipe require a nice glass of Côte du Rhône, it also demands that the cook indulge in a glass (or two!), while stirring, playing music, and quite possibly . . . dancing around the kitchen. There is a secret to this dish that will surprise dinner guests, so be sure to send them to the table to wait while you add the finishing touch! Hidden in each mound of risotto will be a large cube of melty Gorgonzola cheese. Gorgonzola perfectly complements and holds its own ground against the richness of the red wine. The best part is that it is concealed in the center of the dish and is only discovered when one digs a spoon into the risotto and finds a gorgeous nutty and salty creamy center.

SERVES 4 TO 6

6 to 8 cups / 1.5 to 2 L Rich Beef Stock (page 33) or store-bought

2 tablespoons butter

2 tablespoons olive oil

1 medium red onion, thinly sliced

Balsamic vinegar

1½ cups / 300 g arborio rice

1½ cups / 360 ml red wine, ideally Côte du Rhône

5 ounces / 140 g Gorgonzola cheese, about 1 (3 by 3-inch / 7.5 by 7.5 cm) piece for each serving

Salt and freshly ground black pepper

In a large saucepan over medium heat, add the stock. Once the stock is simmering, reduce the heat to low and keep the stock simmering on a back burner.

Set a medium saucepan over medium heat and add the butter and 1 tablespoon of the oil and cook until the butter is melted. Add the onion and slowly cook, until tender and golden. Once you are happy with the color, add a dash of vinegar and as soon as the vinegar has evaporated, remove the onion from the pan using a slotted spoon and set aside.

To the same pot, add the remaining 1 tablespoon oil and the rice. Turn down the heat to medium-low and cook the rice until toasted. You will know this is achieved when the rice begins to smell warm and toasty. Add the wine and pause to enjoy the gorgeous aroma of the steaming wine and the stunning color of the risotto!

Add the hot stock, ladle by ladle, and continue to add more as the liquid is absorbed. Arborio rice can vary quite a bit; some can absorb liquid faster, so adjust your cooking temperature accordingly. I find that risotto needs about 40 minutes to absorb all the liquid and become fully cooked, but I have also had some risotto rice that takes longer. The trick is that you do not want the rice to dry out, and you also do not want the rice to drown in too much stock.

continues >

RED WINE RISOTTO, continued

Once the rice is tender, reheat the caramelized onions in a small pan or with a quick zap in the microwave. Line up shallow dishes or risotto bowls near your risotto pot. You will want to plate the risotto all at once, while it is bubbly hot.

Ladle one large amount of risotto onto the center of each plate. In the center of each, place a block of Gorgonzola. Next, ladle one scoop of hot risotto over each block of cheese, so that it begins to melt and become gooey. Remember, you want to hide the Gorgonzola in the center, so be sure to cover it completely.

To finish the dish, top each plate with the caramelized onions and a drizzle of vinegar. Season with salt and a few turns of pepper to taste.

Daube au Boeuf — Provençal Beef Stew

Provençal daube is a hearty stew that features beef or lamb. Like its Burgundy cousin, boeuf bourguignon, daube features a less-premium cut of meat that benefits from long and low heat in order to be tender. The word daube comes from the Provençal word *adobar*, which means to prepare or marinate in a sauce or liquid. This classic dish is often made in cookware called a *daubière,* a large pot with a sealed rim of paste made from flour and water. A heavy cast-iron covered pot or Dutch oven will also work beautifully for this rich and comforting stew. The addition of root vegetables makes an even heartier meal.

SERVES 4 TO 6

4½ pounds / 2 kg beef chuck, shank, rump, or shoulder

Salt and freshly ground white pepper

6 tablespoons / 90 ml olive oil

½ cup / 100 g lardons or thick-cut smoked bacon, chopped

1 celery stalk, diced

6 small carrots

1 large onion, chopped

1 whole head of garlic, skin on and cut in half

2 tablespoons tomato paste

2 teaspoons salt

1 bottle red wine, such as Côte du Rhône or Bandol

2 to 4 cloves

1 (2 to 3-inch long) strip of orange peel

1 bouquet garni (thyme, bay, and rosemary), or 1 tablespoon herbes de Provence

1 medium leek, quartered

6 to 8 small turnips, quartered

Pasta, for serving

Fresh parsley, for serving

Begin by searing the meat to the point of a golden-brown crust. To achieve this, be sure that the beef is very dry. Dry the meat on all sides with a kitchen towel or paper towels and then sprinkle liberally with salt and white pepper.

In a *daubière* or large Dutch oven over medium-high heat, add 3 tablespoons / 45 ml of the oil. Let the oil get hot before adding the beef. Brown the meat evenly, pressing down with tongs and turning so that all sides are seared. Remove the meat from the pot and set on a platter to rest.

Add the remaining oil to the same pot and begin to sauté the lardons. Add the celery, carrots, and onion and sauté for about 5 minutes to allow the vegetables to fully sweat and begin to become tender. Add the garlic, followed by the tomato paste and 2 teaspoons salt. Add the wine to deglaze the pot and bring to a full boil. Reduce the heat to low and allow the wine to remain at a low boil for 5 more minutes before adding the cloves, orange peel, and bouquet garni. Return the meat to the pot and bring to a simmer.

At the start of the second hour of simmering, add the leek and turnips. The sauce should cook on the stovetop for 2 to 4 hours total. The size of the meat pieces will determine how quickly they will cook. The beef should be tender and fall apart when it is amply cooked. Carefully remove the meat and vegetables and reduce the sauce by continuing to cook on high for an additional 10 to 15 minutes.

Serve the daube over pasta with the sauce ladled on top and sprinkle with the parsley.

Bourride — Fish Soup with Aioli

Bourride is a Provençal fish soup traditionally served with aioli that celebrates the simple rustic flavors of garlic and fennel. White wine is used in the broth, which is thickened by the egg yolks in the aioli. You can use any white fish like sea bass, cod, or whiting for this simple yet elegant traditional soup. *(Pictured on page 276.)*

SERVES 4

FOR THE BROTH

¼ cup / 60 ml olive oil

2 medium onions, coarsely chopped

2 medium leeks, coarsely chopped

1 large bunch of flat-leaf parsley, roughly torn

1 bay leaf

3 tomatoes, quartered

2 garlic cloves, thinly sliced

2 pounds / 900 g fish parts, including bones

1 teaspoon fennel seeds

1½ cups / 360 ml dry white wine

3 cups / 720 ml boiling water

FOR THE SOUP

2 tablespoons olive oil

2 tablespoons butter

½ cup / 80 g finely diced shallots

½ cup / 60 g finely diced celery

½ cup / 60 g finely diced carrots

2 pounds / 900 g white fish, such as cod, sea bass, or whiting, about 1 inch / 2.5 cm thick, cut into 3 to 4-inch / 7.5 to 10 cm pieces

Begin by making the cooking broth. In a large pot over medium heat, warm the oil. Add the onion, leeks, parsley, bay leaf, tomatoes, and garlic. Sauté for a few minutes before adding the fish parts and fennel seeds. Add the wine and water and simmer just under the boil for 10 minutes.

Reduce the heat to a low simmer and continue to warm for 30 minutes. The broth will reduce slightly, so be sure to keep an eye on it so that it doesn't cook down too much. Strain the broth and set aside.

To make the soup, in the same cooking pot over medium heat, add the oil and butter. Once the butter is melted, add the shallots, celery, and carrots. Once the vegetables are becoming tender, add the broth back into the pot before adding the white fish. Over low heat, cook the fish until it is firm and opaque, about 6 to 10 minutes.

FOR SERVING

For garnish—Chopped fresh herbs, such as dill, thyme, or basil (optional)

¾ cup / 150 g cherry tomatoes, halved and lightly salted (optional)

Fennel fronds

Aioli (follows)

Steamed potatoes (optional)

To finish, add chopped fresh herbs, such as dill, thyme, or basil, halved cherry tomatoes, and fennel fronds and serve with aioli as noted below.

There are a few ways you can finish your bourride:

tableside: In France, bourride is sometimes offered with the aioli served in a small bowl on the side and then it is added by spoonful at the table.

as a sauce: You can also remove the fish and then add the aioli to the broth and combine until smooth, simmering until the broth is slightly thickened.

as a stew: Add steamed potatoes to the broth or sauce before serving.

make it fancy: Add fresh herbs, such as dill, thyme, or basil, with the cherry tomatoes.

Aioli

Aioli is an emulsion sauce of garlic and olive oil. Some versions are very close to a traditional mayonnaise and contain egg yolks. In France, Dijon mustard is also frequently added. I prefer to make aioli that is flavorful but not overpowering with garlic. In a well-balanced blend, you should be able to taste not only the garlic but also the mustard, white pepper, and lemon. It's a delicious addition to salads and salad dressings, especially tasty on burgers and sandwiches, and perfect as a dip for veggies. You can make it your own by adding chopped green herbs, such as dill, chives, and basil, chopped olives, sun-dried tomatoes, or capers.

MAKES 2 CUPS / 480 ML

2 garlic cloves

½ teaspoon sea salt

A pinch of white pepper

½ teaspoon Dijon mustard

2 egg yolks

1 teaspoon lemon juice

2 cups / 480 ml olive oil

Using a mortar and pestle, crush the garlic with the salt, pepper, and mustard. Rapidly whisk in the egg yolks with the lemon juice and follow with slow drizzles of oil, until all the ingredients reach full emulsion. You can also use a food processor or electric whisk; just be sure to add the oil very slowly and allow it to thicken before adding more.

Homemade aioli can be kept in an airtight jar or container for up to 1 week in the refrigerator.

° FRANCE
Poireau
2€ 50

° FRANCE
Carotte
2,50 € la botte

Boule aux Herbes de Provence — Herb Bread

If you are daunted by the prospect of bread making, this "no knead" to worry method ensures the perfect crusty boule that is delicious for toast, as an accompaniment for soups and stews, or in a starring role for an evening of bread and cheese. I like to use a light whole wheat bread flour called *semi-complet* in French, but you can use any bread flour that you like.

MAKES 1 LOAF

3 cups / 400 g bread flour, plus more for dusting

1¼ teaspoons salt

¼ teaspoon instant yeast

1⅓ cups / 320 ml tepid water

1 cup / 12 g mixed fresh herbs, such as thyme, rosemary, basil, and oregano, or 1 tablespoon dried herbes de Provence

In a large bowl, combine the flour, salt, yeast, water, and herbs and mix with your hands. The dough mixture will be rough, a bit sticky and clumpy, or "rustic." Cover the bowl with plastic wrap and let sit for 8 hours or overnight at room temperature or, in cooler months, place in an oven that has been turned off.

Turn the dough out onto a floured surface. Dust with extra flour as needed and gently form a ball. Place the dough ball, seam side down, back into the bowl and gently tuck to maintain the round shape. Cover loosely with a damp kitchen towel and let sit for about an hour to rise.

While the dough is proofing, preheat the oven to 450°F / 230°C. Place a large cast-iron Dutch oven in the oven. Let the pot heat thoroughly for 1 hour and then carefully remove the pot from the oven and remove the lid.

Place a sheet of parchment paper on the counter, put the risen dough ball in the center, and then place it in the Dutch oven, leaving the parchment under the dough. Cover the pot and place it in the oven for 30 minutes. After 30 minutes have passed, uncover and continue to bake for 15 to 20 minutes more, until the exterior of the bread is browned and crusty. Cool completely on a wire rack before slicing.

Lemon-Thyme Cake

Thyme is an herb that overwinters in most parts of southern France. It can be pinched for recipes and adds a fresh herbaceous flavor to both savory and sweet dishes. The lemon zest adds brightness to this cake, which pairs well with a cup of tea or a glass of semi-fruity white wine.

MAKES ONE 8-INCH / 20 CM CAKE

1½ cups / 300 g sugar

¾ cup / 165 g salted butter, at room temperature, plus more for greasing the pan

3 large eggs

1¾ cups / 210 g all-purpose flour, plus more for dusting

1 teaspoon baking soda

1 teaspoon baking powder

1 cup / 240 g Greek or full-fat yogurt

Zest from 3 lemons (about 3 tablespoons)

1 bunch of fresh thyme, leaves only, or 2 tablespoons dried thyme. (If using fresh, reserve a few sprigs to decorate the cake.)

Confectioners' sugar, for serving (optional)

Lemon juice, for serving (optional)

Preheat the oven to 350°F / 180°C. Butter an 8 by 4-inch / 20 by 10 cm cake pan. Dust the pan with flour and set aside while you make the batter.

Using a stand mixer or electric hand mixer, cream the sugar and butter until fluffy and well combined, then add the eggs and continue to blend for another minute.

In a medium bowl, combine the flour, baking soda, and baking powder and whisk to fully combine. Gradually add the flour to the bowl with the butter and sugar and beat the batter on medium speed until smooth. Add the yogurt, lemon zest, and finally, the thyme.

Pour the batter into the prepared pan and place the pan in the oven, setting your timer for 45 minutes. Check the cake by inserting a toothpick or a skewer into the center of the cake to check if it is fully cooked. You may need to add more time, checking in 10-minute increments, until the toothpick comes out clean when tested.

Remove the cake from the oven and let it rest on a wire rack for 15 minutes before you turn it onto a plate.

For serving, I love the simplicity of adding a simple dusting of confectioners' sugar and a sprinkling of fresh thyme leaves. You can also make a drizzle of a few tablespoons of confectioners' sugar with a squeeze of fresh lemon juice, if you wish.

Riz au Lait — Creamy Rice Pudding

This creamy and comforting traditional French recipe for rice pudding is made with decadent Pineau-soaked raisins. Pineau is an aperitif of western France that is made from eau-de-vie (a clear fruit brandy) and grape juice that has been aged in oak barrels. The flavor pairs perfectly with golden raisins and adds a festive touch to this classic rice pudding. Cooking times for rice pudding vary based on the type of rice used. In France, we use a long-grain white rice from Camargue commonly used for desserts, which, because of its high starch content, results in a creamy pudding. Cooking until the pudding is creamy and the rice is textured yet soft usually takes an hour at a simmer with Camargue rice.

SERVES 4

6 cups / 1.5 L whole milk

½ cup / 100 g sugar

1 vanilla bean, split

½ cup / 100 g long-grain white rice

¾ cup Pineau (the white version is preferred), cognac, or brandy

½ cup / 70 g golden raisins

½ cup / 80 g dried apricots, chopped

In a large saucepot over medium-high heat, add the milk, sugar, and vanilla bean. Once the milk comes to a low boil, reduce the heat to low and add the rice. Cook for 30 to 60 minutes, until the rice grains are tender and creamy. Again, this will depend on the type of rice used.

Heat the Pineau in a microwave-proof measuring cup for about 30 seconds, then add the raisins and apricot pieces and soak for at least 30 minutes before topping the rice pudding. The dried fruit will become tender and plump and almost fully absorb the Pineau.

Rice pudding can be made days ahead and stored in an airtight container in the refrigerator. Reheat desired portions with a splash of warm cream or milk and ladle into bowls or glasses. The plumped raisins add a special touch, and while some recipes use rum as an alternative, the subtle grape flavor of the Pineau boosts the natural essences of the golden raisins instead of overpowering them.

Poires au Vin Rouge et Épices

Pears Poached in Red Wine and Spices

This simple yet elegant dessert instantly transports you to the feeling of a cozy wool blanket and a crackling fire. Whether it is a crisp winter day or a holiday gathering, this dessert is the perfect end to a meal, especially when one feels there is no room for dessert. The lightly sweetened pears and the dark berry essences from the wine fuse with the warm winter flavors of the spices. The options for creative presentation are almost endless: a teacup, surrounded by the warm spicy wine, or propped elegantly on a saucer, wreathed in a large pool of Crème Anglaise (page 286) with a bay leaf peeking out of the stem of the pear. *Le mélange d'épices à vin chaud* is a blend of holiday spices found during Christmastime and features cloves, allspice, anise, and nutmeg. You can purchase the mixture preblended and use a simple tea sachet to infuse into the wine or make a mixture using the ingredients noted below.

SERVES 6

1 bottle dry red wine, such as Côte du Rhône

1½ cups / 300 g sugar

2 large bay leaves, plus 6 small, fresh ones, for garnish

1 cinnamon stick

2 sachets *les épices du vin chaud*, or ¼ teaspoon each of ground cloves, allspice, anise, and nutmeg

6 medium pears, firm with stem intact, carefully peeled

Crème Anglaise (page 286), for serving

In a saucepan deep enough for the pears to be completely submerged in the wine over medium-high heat, combine the wine and sugar and heat until the sugar is dissolved. Add the 2 bay leaves and cinnamon stick along with the sachets and bring to a full boil for 1 minute.

Reduce the heat to low and gently add the pears to the warm wine mixture. I find that it is best to simmer the wine and pears without a cover. This allows for the wine to slightly reduce and lessens the chance of overcooking the pears. Simmer for about 30 minutes, checking every 15 minutes by poking a pear with a toothpick or the tip of a paring knife.

Cook until tender but not too soft, so the pears hold their shape and remain pretty for serving. If you are making these a day ahead, you can place the entire pan, covered, in the refrigerator. Otherwise, I just move the pan to the back of the stove and allow the pears to come to room temperature, while I make the rest of the meal.

You can serve the pears in a bowl with the infused wine or set them on a paper towel to dry before standing them in a shallow dish of crème anglaise. Poke a bay leaf through the top of each pear to garnish.

Crème Anglaise

Crème anglaise is a simple custard used as a pudding or as a silky, lightly sweet sauce that requires only four ingredients—egg yolks, milk, sugar, and vanilla. It pairs perfectly with almost any dessert, enhances the flavor of dark chocolate, and counters the tartness of fruit coulis.

MAKES 2 CUPS / 480 ML

2 cups / 480 ml whole milk

½ cup / 100 g sugar

6 egg yolks

1½ teaspoons vanilla extract

In a medium heavy-bottomed saucepan over medium heat, add the milk and ¼ cup / 100 g of the sugar. Simmer until the mixture just starts to bubble. Remove the pan from the heat and let stand for 20 minutes.

Meanwhile, in a medium bowl, whisk the egg yolks with the remaining ¼ cup / 100 g of the sugar along with the vanilla. To temper the sauce and prevent the egg yolks from scrambling, spoon some of the hot cream mixture into the egg yolk mixture, then swiftly whisk to combine. Add another spoon of the infused milk to the eggs, until the egg mixture is warm to the touch. Finally, pour the tempered cream and egg mixture into the remaining cream in the saucepan and return the pan to the heat.

Continue to cook over medium heat while constantly stirring, until the custard coats the back of a spoon; this will take about 5 minutes.

Once the custard has thickened, remove the pan from the heat and strain through a fine-mesh sieve into a medium bowl to remove any lumps. Allow the custard to cool before ladling into a small pitcher for serving. The custard can be kept in in a covered jar in the refrigerator for up to 1 week.

Galette des Rois — King Cake

In our family, a galette des rois has several levels of importance. Not only is it served in recognition of the Feast of the Epiphany in early January, but as two of my three children have birthdays at that time, they will sometimes have it as their birthday cake! The cake traditionally contains a small porcelain *fève*, which is a hand-painted ceramic figurine hidden in the frangipane, the almond cream filling. The finder of the *fève* (watch out when taking a bite!) will be the king for the day and wears a paper crown that accompanies the cake.

SERVES 6

FOR THE FILLING

1½ cups / 200 g blanched almonds

⅔ cup / 130 g sugar

½ cup plus 2 tablespoons / 150 g salted butter, melted

2 large eggs, lightly beaten

⅛ teaspoon (just a few drops) almond extract

1 (16-ounce / 450 g) package of all-butter puff pastry sheets

Flour, for rolling out pastry, as needed

1 large egg yolk, beaten, for sealing and glazing the pastry

Preheat the oven to 375°F / 190°C.

To make the filling, add the almonds and sugar to a food processor and pulse until they form a grainy flour texture. Add in the butter, eggs, and almond extract. Take care when adding the almond extract, since it can be quite potent and you only want a subtle hint of almond flavoring.

Line a baking sheet with parchment paper.

If frozen, thaw the pastry per the instructions provided. Roll out the pastry into two 12-inch / 30 cm circles on parchment paper or a floured surface. Place one circle on the prepared baking sheet and spread the pastry with an even layer of the filling, leaving a ½-inch / 1.5 cm margin around the edge. If you have a *fève* to add, push it gently into the filling. Cover with the second circle and seal the edges of the pastry with some of the egg yolk. Crimp the edges closed with the tines of a fork and then use a very sharp knife to cut a pattern into the top of the pastry. Glaze with the remaining egg yolk and bake for 30 minutes until evenly golden-brown.

Remove the pan from the oven and cool on a wire rack for 15 minutes before serving.

Pain d'Épices — Spice Bread

Pain d'épices is the French equivalent of gingerbread and dates back to the 17th century. Requisite ingredients are rye flour, honey, and spices in this lightly sweet cake. In France, it is often eaten with a touch of cold butter for *goûter*, afternoon snack time, but it can also be served as a dessert, served with sweetened whipped cream or vanilla ice cream.

MAKES ONE 9-INCH / 23 CM ROUND CAKE OR AN 8 BY 4-INCH / 20 BY 10 CM LOAF

¼ cup / 60 g unsalted butter, at room temperature, plus more for buttering the pan

3½ cups / 420 g all-purpose flour

½ cup / 60 g rye flour

2½ teaspoons baking soda

1½ teaspoons ground ginger

1½ teaspoons ground cinnamon

½ teaspoon salt

¼ teaspoon ground nutmeg

¼ teaspoon ground cloves

¼ teaspoon freshly ground black pepper

½ teaspoon whole anise seeds

1 large egg

1 cup / 340 g honey

⅓ cup / 60 g loosely packed dark brown sugar

1 tablespoon finely grated orange zest

1 cup / 240 ml whole milk

Preheat the oven to 325°F / 160°C. Butter a 9-inch / 23 cm round cake pan or an 8 by 4-inch / 20 by 10 cm loaf pan.

In a large glass bowl, combine the flours, baking soda, ginger, cinnamon, salt, nutmeg, cloves, pepper, and anise seeds.

Using a stand mixer with the whisk attachment, cream the butter, egg, honey, and brown sugar, then add the orange zest and milk. Slowly incorporate the dry ingredients and mix until uniformly combined.

Pour the batter into the prepared pan and bake for 45 minutes. Insert a skewer into the center of the cake to test for doneness. The top should be golden and dry, and the skewer should come out clean when the batter is fully cooked through. The cake is traditionally dense and somewhat dry in texture. Allow to cool before slicing.

Gâteau à l'Orange — Orange Cake

One of the cakes I make in the winter season is a rustic, textured orange cake sometimes called whole orange cake. It is similar to an Italian olive-oil cake in its density and use of almond meal. The orange offers a vibrant citrus flavor and a stunning color. Best of all, it only requires five basic ingredients and can be completely gluten-free. Organic, unwaxed citrus is recommended, as all parts of the orange will be used for the recipe. This cake is a lovely treat for your afternoon tea. Serve with fresh orange slices, or simply dusted with powdered sugar.

MAKES ONE 9-INCH / 23 CM ROUND CAKE

2 medium oranges (about 10 ounces / 280 g each)

Butter, for buttering the pan

1¼ teaspoons baking powder

6 large eggs at room temperature

1¼ cups / 250 g sugar

2⅔ cup / 300 g almond meal (almond flour made from blanched and peeled almonds can also be used)

Wash the oranges, place them in a medium pot, and cover completely with water. Bring the water to a boil over medium-high heat and then reduce the heat to medium and continue to boil for 30 minutes. After 30 minutes, gently poke the peels. The oranges should be plump and the peel should be easy to poke through with the tip of a knife.

Remove from heat and place the oranges on a cutting board to cool. Preheat the oven to 325°F / 160°C. Butter a 9-inch / 23 cm diameter round cake pan.

Once the oranges are cool enough to handle, cut each of the oranges into eighths, removing the seeds and then scrape the orange pieces and juices on the cutting board into a food processor. Process the oranges until they become a semi-smooth paste.

Add the baking powder, eggs, sugar, and almond meal to the food processor and blitz for 15 seconds. Scrape down the sides of the bowl if necessary and blitz for a few more seconds before pouring the batter into the prepared cake pan. Bake for 60 minutes until the cake is a deep golden brown and a skewer poked into the center of the cake comes out clean.

Cool the cake for 20 to 25 minutes before inverting it on a plate. The cake stores well in an airtight container for up to 5 days at room temperature, or in a sealed container in the refrigerator for up to 2 weeks. It also freezes beautifully wrapped in parchment paper and foil or plastic wrap and can be stored frozen up to 3 months.

ARRIVING IN A NEW COUNTRY IS LIKE cooking in someone else's kitchen. You might know the ingredients and the techniques, but the rest, such as finding the right tools and using a different oven, can be enough to turn even a familiar dish into a disappointment. It was important for my integration into this new life to learn everything I could about French cuisine, in part, to stretch myself and expand my knowledge as a foodie and in larger part, to honor a family that I was so eager to be accepted by.

I was determined to fully integrate and embrace their culture instead of forcing my own. But I think there were several things I didn't fully understand or could not have predicted, the most significant being my struggle to master the language. While many have said that within months, you will be fluent when you move to a new country, I wasn't. I also wasn't prepared that people would be kind about that failure for only a short time. I was given a grace-period for not speaking French, but once that had expired, I soon learned how devastating it was to my sense of belonging not only to be unable to communicate with professionals like doctors and businesspeople, even more important, with my French family.

So, I used mastering French cuisine and feeding people as my language. At first, my classroom was my father-in-law's kitchen, where I sat quietly and shyly observed. Then I explored local markets as a regular ritual. I expanded my relationships with producers and growers.

A new life in a new place. In looking back to that long-ago morning on a windy beach, where I had my destiny-altering conversation with God, I realize that it was there, when I chose to firmly plant my feet in French soil. It was there, where I made a promise: that I would handle anything that came my way with *grace*. I was ready for what lay ahead—a home, a new beginning, and experiences that would create the stories that would weave the fabric of our family.

But for all of this to come together, there had to be a kitchen, and before that a home. I soon learned that for a kitchen to fully come to life, it takes more than carefully selected ingredients and recipes, culinary tools, and a stove. A kitchen is a place of comfort, where people can find a safe haven when comfort is scarce. It's a place where you can raise your voice, whisper a prayer, and continue to build your dreams, and on the more difficult days, to save them.

As much as we hosted neighbors and new friends in our first little house in Normandy, it wasn't until we created our kitchen at Rabbit Hill that our new life took root. We made a home that we never could have dreamed of, a place to watch our kids grow, see gardens thrive and fail, and animals born and raised.

And maybe most importantly, a kitchen where more than just delicious meals were made. Countless lessons of grace would be taught in the space of four walls, through tall windows and the beautiful light they let in. It was there we learned to persevere through countless adjustments and trials and to celebrate immeasurable moments of joy together. It remains a place to embrace the seasons, honor the past, savor the present, and chart the future.

Fin.

ACKNOWLEDGMENTS — MERCI

I AM SO HONORED to be able to create not only a book of recipes, but also share lessons from a special kitchen and the life it encouraged. I have been blessed with the opportunity to create and live in an amazing and richly beautiful place of food, culture, tradition, and family.

I want to begin by thanking my family. I could not have done this book without the constant reminder that everything is possible on a strong foundation that consists of "us five." To Maxim, my oldest, my humor, my friend— thank you for endless hours of encouragement, reading proofs, and always good laughs. To Leo, thanks for being steady and those priceless jabs that kept me going. Lily—my girl. For believing that your mom is amazing even if it meant less time and less focus than you deserve. So much goodness and beauty ahead for you and us! For "*mon amour*" . . . I can't even measure the level of what you have had to put up with due to my angsty, artsy, creative side. But I do cook a great meal! And speaking of that—thanks for eating the same dish several times a week while I sorted out recipes. Thanks for standing by when all I wanted was "wine for dinner" and being willing to order pizza. Thank you, family, for giving me the time and space to work on this dream.

Mom and Dad, little did you know that someday your daughter would head off to parts unknown and try to survive a new culture and language barrier. Thanks for trying countless dishes, for traveling so far so often, for your steady faithful prayers, and for always being there during the hard moments, little victories, and all of the in-between. Thank you for raising me to be who I am.

Significant acknowledgment and a bottomless cup of thanks to the beautiful and fierce women in my life. I could not have completed this project without you. To Amy, Laura, Meg, and Sandrine . . . You cheered me on not from the sidelines, but from within arm's reach. You inspire me and challenge me and I can't imagine having done this without you. Your kindness, encouragement, wisdom, and more than all that—friendship—is everything to me.

A very special thanks to another beauty— Erin. The day I sent you a message—you responded in minutes, saying " . . . the world needs this book!" I would not have done this book without you believing in me from that very first moment.

Thank you to everyone that has passed through our home and stood in my kitchen. You listened and laughed, learned and shared, and gave. Through the years I have been so blessed to gather with you around a table.

I am so grateful for the team at Highline Literary Collective, Kim and Margaret, and Hardie Grant—North America. Thank you for giving me incredible insight and expertise to create the best book possible. I could not have done this book without Jenny Wapner, my editor, who confidently took me on and provided support and enthusiasm throughout the project. I am so grateful and honored to have benefited from such incredible talent and professionalism during this process.

Hardie Grant

NORTH AMERICA

2912 Telegraph Ave
Berkeley, CA 94705
hardiegrantusa.com

Published in the United States
by Hardie Grant North America,
an imprint of Hardie Grant
Publishing Pty Ltd.

Library of Congress
Cataloging-in-Publication Data
is available upon request.

ISBN: 9781958417393
ISBN: 9781958417409 (eBook)
Printed in CHINA

First Edition